Derelict Days . . .

Sixty years on the Roadside Path to Enlightenment

Irv Thomas

With a recently discovered account of
The First American Hitch-hiker

First published by AuthorHouse 09/27/04

ISBN: 1-4184-7010-4 (e)
ISBN: 1-4184-2964-3 (sc)

Library of Congress Control Number: 2004092959

Printed in the United States of America
Bloomington, Indiana

This book is printed on acid-free paper.

By the same Author:

Innocence Abroad: Adventuring through Europe at 64 on $100 per week

Dedicated

to the *Free Spirit* hiding within each,
that tempts us, teases us, and finally
lures the fortunate few
to the Open Road;

and also to the *Community Spirit*
that moves the willing driver
to make a connection

with the *Free Spirit*

Proceeds from the sale of this book are going toward
the support of
The Road Bard Project
(www.roadbard.org)

Contents

* These are life-hitch tales, each recounting a passage of years.

12.3 The Geriatric Hitch-hiker ... at 82

Foreword

by Morgan 'Sal'man Strub (Facilitator of the Road Bard Project)

The idea seemed a simple one. Gather up the hitch-hikers of North America to meet on a November weekend in Seattle. Bernd Wechner, a longtime champion of the travel mode, was flying in from Australia. Word was that a wizened old man of the road named Irv lived in the city and might be persuaded to join us. And so we were three.

The year before I had begun a website for hitch-hikers called digihitch.com. Its purpose was to bring together the stories and resources of the road, to create a community of ourselves out of a shared understanding and larger journey. Bernd was an editor on the subject of hitch-hiking at Suite101.com. His monthly articles and call to connect inspired me to take it further, to create an interactive portal where every voice and piece of wisdom gleaned from the road can be heard.

Bernd told me of Irv's website, and there I was first introduced to the soulful world of a kindred traveler. His stories held the weight of one who has not only lived an extraordinary life, but also trusted and trudged a road less traveled.

In November, on a cold but surprisingly sunny day in Seattle, I met Irv Thomas. The years and miles had been kind to him, shining brightly in his eyes and winking smile. By way of his writings I was prepared to like him, but I had not expected to so strongly relate to him. Here was a man of 75 strong years. As he told his story to a writer from Seattle Times who had joined us, I found myself nodding and sparking with resonance.

The road and its symbols have shaped us both, I thought. There must be so many more of us out there!

The hitch-hiker gathering had rounded up only a handful. Sitting in a park on the edge of Seattle, we shared stories and sipped hot drinks. Wonderfully unexpected, a man who had recently hitch-hiked through Central America overheard our conversation while cycling through the park. As he joined us, we spoke of the serendipities of the road.

There was an excited buzz among us, the feeling that we were waking to a common thread long forgotten. Were the hitch-hikers out there? Did they see the thread? There was no doubt. I had met them at the crossroads of America, read their stories across the Web.

Among hitch-hikers there is already an incredible community of writers, artists, musicians and craftspeople. Hitch-hiking is itself a creative process, where each leg of the trip and personal connection shapes the destination – and sense of arrival.

Traveling I-90 to New York, a few years back, I met two fellow hitch-hikers in Rapid City, South Dakota. Next morning we would depart in opposite directions, but that night we sat in a field and sang songs of the road as the musician among us strummed his guitar. It was a shared experience that bolstered me for the hundreds of miles ahead, an energy I could impart to each driver along the way.

Hitch-hikers who hear the music have become like the traveling minstrels of older times, imparting glad tidings, open possibility and a sense of adventure. It is in that spirit that the

Road Bard project was formed, and for which we are honored to have Irv as a founding member.

The Road Bard project will encourage travelers to participate in the communities through which they pass, lending their ear, voice and talent – even muscle – where needed. It will also work to foster relationships with other organizations, creating a vital path and personal rapport from one beacon to the next.

There are three song-filled travelers who embody the spirit of the Road Bard. They are Walt Whitman, Woody Guthrie and Irv Thomas. As his stories and recollections show, Irv has invited providence and purpose along each leg of the journey. I – for one – am grateful, and the thread remains to be shared.

Morgan 'Sal'man Strub
Hitch-hiker, Road Bard

Bouquets . . . and a Razzberry

Though writing is always a solo effort, the publication of a book is just as always not. For this one, there are a few people to thank: Morgan Strub and Krista Arias for stirring me to it, in the first place, by turning up in town with their flash of invigorating confidence in the existence of an open-road host and energy in this otherwise dreary new millennium; David Blatner, ever the faithful computer resource; Farrell Winter for the single on-the-road photo of me that I could put my hands on; Maureen Taylor, Joy Cutting, Betsy Buck and Evelyn Drevet for four other views of me at momentary points along the road; and Alice Joy, my constant and reliable auditioning ear and appraising eye (among many other things she is to me), who never lets me down.

Speaking of which – being let down – the single razzberry goes to a certain sub-editor on the Portland Oregonian (who shall remain nameless) for his indelicate suggestion of an impossible price to allow the use of a truly neat photo of me they once printed — thus depriving you of my beaming radiance in a book where it properly belongs.

Prelude

(How it came to be my) Avocation: Hitch-Hiking

One sunny February afternoon in the first year of our new millennium, the day's mail held a rather surprising letter — a formal request for my biographical specs from the A.N.Marquis people, publishers of *Who's Who in America.*

It struck me as a marvelously delightful joke. *Who's Who* had always been, for me, the testament to achievement in the world of movers and shakers, going as far back as my memory of library resources. While outranked by such as Pulitzers and Oscars, perhaps, it nevertheless was up there in the Pantheon: a catalog of people who had made it, Big Time. My letter of invitation might not have been intended as a joke, but it was certainly one *Big Time goof.*

I mean, I had accomplished a few things in my three recent decades as a writer, and maybe things a bit out of the ordinary, but not the stuff of serious recognition. Over the years, I'd put out a couple of off-beat 'sporadicals' – what they'd call zines, today – made sundry presentations at a few national conferences, done some mostly ineffective social activism on the local scene, and had one lone book to my name. Hardly the 'what's what' of *Who's Who* caliber. My life has just lacked the focused self-discipline that drives folks to such status.

But I thought it would be fun to play the game through, so I filled out their bio-questionnaire with what I could put into it. So sure was I that my submission would go directly into their discard file, that when I came to the final question, as to my avocation, I gave in to an instant impulse and put down "hitch-hiking." I figured it would at least leave them smiling.

At the time, I was just about to put an issue of *Ripening Seasons*, my sporadical of the moment, into the postal stream, and so I added this short mention of the strange development at the end of it . . .

> There is one more rather unusual sprout that I have to tell you about, before closing this Spring Equinox report. I'm not even sure quite what to make of it, but it arrived at the proper time and, notwithstanding the absurdity of it, has got to have some sort of meaning. It was a great head-bender, I'll tell you!

...the "proper time" being early February, when things portentous of the year's activity always seem to sprout in my haphazard world.

In due course, and to my serious amazement, the 'sprout' did, indeed, grow and bear fruit, and I've been listed in *Who's Who* ever since — with the avocation of hitch-hiking. Without doubt, it is the only such characterization in their two thick volumes and nearly 6000 pages, filled with far more significant people than I am.

Well, I had never considered my hitch-hiking an avocation — though it has been many other things to me, over the course of my sixty years' indulgence. To begin with, it was just a school kid's vacation lark at 16, and a way of stretching my boundaries of geographic familiarity. Then, for awhile, it became an agreeably cheap way of visiting distant friends, spiced with a bit of reliably dicey adventure. But I thought I had fully done with it by my early 20s, when I proceeded to 'get serious about life,' as I might have said in those days.

It was twenty more years or so, before I returned to the roadside with a thumb stuck out — but not exactly for the same old reasons. I was now done with living 'seriously' (in a conventional sense). It had gained me little of what I wanted from life — more grief, by far, than satisfaction. So I walked out of it when in my mid-40s. Rather literally, for one thing I left behind was the ownership of a vehicle. It was too costly to maintain in my new mode of life. I returned to hitch-hiking as simply one of the options in my newly-framed world of low-cost transportation.

And so it was, for the first few years of my revitalizing, until I began to see in hitch-hiking subtleties I had never noticed before. There was a clearly undeniable sense of synchronicity about it, in the way my road trips – short or long – seemed to develop. I began to see linkages, like chain reactions that related one ride to the next, and both of them to still another. It became instructive of life, in ways I hadn't before noticed.

Soon, it became a rolling demonstration of some natural Providence at work in our lives — something we are never aware of while we live lives that are largely predictable and arranged in advance. For hitch-hiking can't possibly be arranged in advance. And then I found myself going out on the road for the sheer 'high' of the experience — an observer as much as a participant, in this strange adventure that continually revealed facets of some Universal Order, never failing to teach and astound me.

Any thinking, inquisitive person confronted with such fascinating revelations cannot help but contemplate what is being revealed about life, itself — and before long, to consider applying those perceptions as deliberately to life, itself, as one sets out deliberately to seek the blessings of the open road. Maybe tepidly at first, but as the Providence becomes routinely evident, then with an increasing gusto and a full willingness to risk the outcome. The ultimate effect might be called a hitch-hiking approach to life: *Let it happen*, and take your cues from the way it happens.

This is not easily done in our routinely structured world. Every nerve-ending in our safety-softened body, every synapse junction in our security-focused brain balks at the very suggestion. But we didn't evolve by precautionary living, nor by hanging back for lack of certainty. These are merely habits we've gotten used to, encouraged by a commercial world that profits on our cautious hesitation. To begin with, we were creatures of chance, and have strayed too far from those roots.

My life changed radically once more, when I put these insights into practice. I left my relatively secure (if entirely alternative) Northern California world behind, and ventured first to the Northwest – taking things just as they came – and finally overseas to Europe, for a 19-month adventure which fully validated my notion that life is most richly lived in a hitch-hiking motif.

I've already written a book on that fabulous experience . . . *Innocence Abroad: Adventuring through Europe at 64 on $100 per week*. Several hitch-hiking tales from it have been included here (see Sections 9 and 10). These, and most of the rest in this book, were written within months of the hitch-hikes chronicled, when the road trips – whether a hundred miles or a thousand – were fresh and real for me. Some were written for *Ripening Seasons*, others for an earlier sporadical, *Black Bart* or its derivative newsletters, and one was intended (never made it) for *Mother Earth News*.

But the book is essentially chronological, starting way back in my life, and the opening tales in Section 1 have only the freshness of happy recollection. I did write them up at the time, but that time was some 60 years ago, and many baggage losses since. Nevertheless, the parts of those trips I do recall remain remarkably 'present' for me and I've chosen not to fudge what I don't actually remember. I only ask that you excuse the lost gaps between those passages.

The book's organization is best visualized in its Contents page. There are twelve Sections, seven of which are entire tales, the remaining five each incorporating two or three individuated tales, or Episodes as I've called them, on some common thematic basis, be it only a timeframe. Among the entire 19 tales in the book, three of them – indicated by asterisk in the Contents page – are more than road-hitching tales. They span a time of years, each, and are included as illuminations of what personal experience can be like when the hitch-hiking motif has become a way of life. You can think of them as *life-hitching* tales, and they underscore the claim I make that hitch-hiking is a roadside path to enlightenment.

I have annotated the tales to provide each with a context, which should make up for the lack of a strict continuity. You'll find these contexting passages at the start of each Section, either for an individual tale or a cluster of them, as may be the case. Since the book is more about the way of the open road than its particular geography, I've felt it necessary to include only a few maps where they help to explain situations in possibly unfamiliar territory. And since the work is essentially autobiographical, I've also incorporated personal photographs that indicate the changes I've come through, across the years.

As a final offering, I've included something special: a tale of an earlier road trip than any of mine. It may well be the story of the very first intentional hitch-hiking ever done in this country — I'm sure it is the earliest of known record. It came to light shortly before this book was ready to be sent to press, and is reprinted here for the first time, to my knowledge, in 87 years.

Without a single other intervening paragraph, now, I welcome you to these tales of my life.

Irv Thomas
Seattle, 2004.

Section 1

Kid stuff (1943-45)

Hitch-hiking begins as an inexpensive and adventurous way of travel. Fortunate is he (or sometimes she) whose world and spirit are free enough for the undertaking, for it is best done with an open mind and an unhurried sense of time.

I was 16 when I started and the country was in the midst of a war, which happened to make it easier for me, as hitch-hiking was enjoying one of its periodic vogues. Maybe I could even claim an earlier start, harking back to 1938 when my mother led a family expedition down the coast highway on a walk to sample an early west coast youth hostel recently opened in Montara.

But I didn't actively seek a ride on that occasion, I merely grabbed an offer from a passing motorist who had pulled up, wondering if I was lost.

Heck, no, I was only lagging behind the main entourage by a few hundred yards. Nevertheless, I was quick to accept the ride, from which I very shortly debarked with a self-satisfied grin of glory, anticipating at the very least a commendation for my cleverness. What I got instead was a shocked reaction of motherly disapproval, emphasized with a stern directive to "Never do that again!"

And I have to say now that I broke my word of assent many times over, through the years — resulting, happily, in no further parental consternation.

1

Here are two of those occasions — the aforementioned journey at age 16, and a subsequent one two years later, each of which took me about a thousand miles from home and opened whole new worlds for me. These are recollected tales, written recently for a forthcoming work of autobiography, so they may lack the fresh perspective of recent experience to be found in most of the book's remaining material. In fact, I cannot be sure that all the events told in the second tale are from one journey, as I traveled southward more than once that year and may have conflated the various experiences.

But time's process has filtered out most of the dross, and certified for me what was really memorable of those early road experiences. Like the pre-freeway pleasure of really open highways – especially for those of us on foot – and a pace of driving at which faces could be seen and their expressions noted, as the cars passed by. And I could hardly forget the wonderful clarity of the air, in the times before smog.

Yes, a few of us old roadies can remember hitching in the time before smog! Don't eat your heart out over it, but be aware that it might have been that way, once. And take my word, it was.

Episode 1.1

My First Night in Jail

B ack in the days when the world was still young, and
reasonably happy, and I was a high school kid, I worked a
summer job as a mail clerk with an outfit called Postal Telegraph
— hardly remembered, nowadays, but once the major competitor
to Western Union. It was 1943, and we were in the midst of a
great war, but we had a government that was fairly true to its
expressed principles, in those happier days . . . or maybe happy
times are just part of being young.

At any rate, so it was — and when my job came to its
summer's end, I found I had a couple weeks of vacation time still
left, and money that – as Mom used to say – was burning a hole
in my pocket. I could afford a real vacation with it, and had an
idea that had been bubbling around in my head for weeks.

Guys in uniform hardly more than my age were getting
rides, here and there, around the country, by hitch-hiking. It
was patriotic to pick them up and help them along their way,
and I saw no reason why I couldn't take advantage of the same
generosity. I had no uniform, of course, but maybe I could fool a

3

few drivers into thinking I did, long enough to get them to stop for me. Sixteen years old, now, I should be able to pull it off.

I went to a big army surplus store on Market Street, up near Van Ness, that sold old military gear for pretty cheap and bought me a khaki jacket that fit fairly well and a pair of pants to go with it, both for less than four dollars. I also picked up a G.I. water canteen that struck me as a good idea.

That was about all I figured I needed that I didn't already have. I was going to head for the Canadian border, going through territory I'd never seen. I had very vague memories of a trip north that the whole family took when I probably wasn't more than 3 or 4 years old; but outside of that, I hadn't been anywhere north of San Francisco farther than the Russian River, about 50 miles away.

I was going to take a little .25 caliber Spanish automatic with me, that I had bargained down, for, to $7 from a friend in school. It was small enough to fit in my jacket pocket, and who knows what I might run into on a trip like this. But Dad talked me out of it. I told him it was just in case I should be attacked by a bear, or something, but he said if I shot a bear with a .25 I'd be in worse trouble than if I didn't. Besides, what if I was picked up by the police for impersonating a serviceman — which would be bad enough, without having a gun to explain.

He was right, I guess. As usual, he came up with arguments I couldn't beat. I didn't really expect I'd run into a bear, but it was all that I could think of when he wanted to know why.

By the time I hit the road, I had about ten days before school opened, and I figured that should be enough to get up there and back. I took a bus to Vallejo, to get started, because it took me right out of all the local traffic and cost only 75¢. But I made sure it was a Sacramento bus, because they make a rest stop right on the highway, at Terry's, instead of going into town to

4

the bus depot there. Terry's is a big restaurant that just about everyone stops at, after the long ride through all the small towns to get out of the Bay Area, so it was also a good place to start my hitching from.

I no longer recall most of the detail of that road trip, but some of what I do remember of it has a clarity that makes it seem like hardly last month. Much of it revolves around the way I spent my nights, for it hadn't occurred to me to get a sleeping bag. Maybe I thought it would detract from the image of the home-bound soldier I was trying to create. Whatever the reason, it became the big challenge, every time nightfall rolled around, and left me with some of the richest memories of that adventure.

The first night was easy. I had gotten a ride with a Butte county civil service employee – a draftsman, as I recall – who lived in Oroville, the county seat. He not only took me home with him for dinner, but allowed me a cot with a blanket out on their porch, where I got a good night's sleep. It was perfect luck, for it showered during the night, and I stayed snugly dry. I hung around town a bit in the morning to give the day some time for clearer skies.

It wasn't much improved, however, by the time I got a ride in the back of a stake truck that had been carrying sheep. But a mixed blessing it was — I thought it best to stand in the truck for the whole of the twenty-mile ride, because I was leery of staining my pants with what was all over the truck bed. A flash of that is forever imprinted on me: patchy sunlight breaking through fragmented clouds of intense whites and grays, bringing the greens all around to equal brilliance, as the mix of fresh and muggy air so typical of very recent rain blended right in with the field scent of alfalfa and the pungent 'deposit' under my feet. I was unimaginably happy in this strange mix of sensory stimuli, as we rumbled up the valley.

I didn't get very far that day, maybe because I stopped short in Redding, to get a fresh morning start at tackling the mountains that lay directly across the river. It was the last town of any consequence before Oregon, still a hundred miles away, and I just wasn't sure what I'd run into in the mountains. I wanted a full day for it.

Redding wasn't much, in those days. The highway went right through town on its main street, straight as a bee line to the same Sacramento River as – though it was significantly smaller than – the Sacramento that flows far to the south, by the city that shares its name. Walking down the west side of that main street, I came to a cottage just being built. Almost finished, it appeared to offer a perfectly good shelter for the night. I went on, to see the rest of the town and get a bite of food, but I returned before darkness set in, and everything worked like a charm. An old newspaper spread nicely into a perfectly good blanket, and I got a pretty good sleep, not in any way affected by more of those late-night showers.

I guess it took me all the next day to get through the mountains, and while I remember nothing of the rides I had, the beauty of the rock formations around Dunsmuir – and that picturesque little railroad town, itself, huddled on a hillside above a tumbling river – made a lasting impression. Awed, as well, by Mt. Shasta beyond, I was having the best possible vacation I could have chosen.

Then came the state border crossing into Oregon, the first time in conscious memory I had ever been outside of California. Oregon had strangely flat-topped prominences, called table mountains, like nothing I had ever seen. That evening found me walking along the highway between Medford and Grant's Pass, enjoying the countryside, even though there were some visible forest fires on the nearby mountain slopes to the south. But people didn't seem much concerned about it. At least, I didn't see any fuss being made.

It was so warm that night, that I figured I could just sleep fully outdoors, with no problem There was an almost full moon to show the way, and I just kept walking until it seemed pretty late, before settling down and getting comfortable under a big tree. But it fooled me. It was cold when I woke up, and pitch dark — the moon had set. So I just lay there getting colder, for the hour or so it took until I could see enough to resume the now-chilly walk toward Grant's Pass. I finally got a ride for the remaining distance and found myself some hot breakfast, resolving as I ate that I would never again imagine I could spend a whole night out of doors — no matter *how* warm it seemed to be.

With the early start, I made it all the way through Oregon that day, and well into Washington — though I remember almost nothing of it. I do have a funny recollection of coming out of the mountains directly into Roseburg, and the car I was riding in had a bit too much speed for the tight left turn into the town's first street. He clipped the curb and blew out his right front tire.

It's probably hard to imagine, for those who never experienced the pre-freeway years, what it was like when major highways were two-lane, curvy roads that came abruptly into towns — absolutely never bypassing any of them, and most usually on the main street. Part of driving cross-country in those days was the invariably sudden shift from one kind of driving to another with never much warning, and no reliable transition zone.

I was actually making pretty good time, considering that it had been almost entirely mountain travel since Redding. In mountain driving, on even the best roads of that day, a car could seldom average more than 35 miles per hour. Every tight turn had to be slowed for, and horns honked when it really got curvy, just to make sure any oncoming driver knew you were coming.

I remember nothing of Portland, but I have a very good recall of Olympia in Washington, where I spent that next night. With every night, now, a challenge, I considered myself especially clever in the way I handled it in Olympia.

As with most towns, the highway came right down the main street to a T-fork at its base. And in the first block to the right of that T was a used-car lot, its wire-link fence and gate locked for the night. But there was no one around, and I had no difficulty scaling that fence — on the gamble that a car door inside would be open. And one was. So I had a fairly comfortable sleep that night in the back seat of an automobile – I can still conjure, after all these years, the sensory mustiness of its cushioned rear seat! – and I was safely over the fence and on my way again, before 7 a.m. next morning.

I zipped through Seattle, as I had Portland, very intent now on getting to my border destination. But the rides suddenly stalled on a hot and barren stretch of roadway outside of Mt. Vernon, seemingly a stone's throw from my goal. It looked like I wasn't going to get beyond that point, for what reason I cannot guess. With an early awareness of the stupidity of fixations, I told myself that for all practical purposes I had met the challenge that I took on, and with hardly a twinge of regret, I walked across the two-lane highway and started hitching homeward.

I definitely remember Seattle on the return. I remember a long street in the heart of town, and overnight occupancy rates that would not overshoot my budget now that the return was underway. I had actually taken about $75 with me for the journey, not knowing what to expect, and I still had almost $50 left, so I could well afford to ease up on my restraint. But caution was still the keynote, so what I finally went for was the cheapest I could find: a dorm room at 50¢ per bed, for the night.

Besides me, five other takers were in the same room, the six cots laid out with hardly any space to spare. The linen seemed clean, if a bit threadbare, but that's about all you could say for the place. My five 'roommates' presented a uniform picture of having lived beyond their prime — if, indeed, they'd ever had a prime. None of them spoke among themselves, they just laid their outer clothing on the chairs provided, so I did the same and crawled into bed.

Before the last one turned the lights out, the guy in the cot next to mine said, "Kid?"

And I responded, "Yeah?"

"You better not leave your wallet in your pants. Put it under your pillow or something."

I don't know whether he'd been watching me, or just decided I could use the advice, but it was a good suggestion and I immediately removed my wallet and put it under my pillow.

I slept pretty soundly, and when I finally awoke it was full daylight and I was the only one remaining in the room. The first thing I did was to lift my pillow — but there was no wallet under it!

I searched all around the cot and under it, but it was just gone. Jeez! Had I been played for a sucker by that guy with the good advice? He's the one who knew *exactly* where to look, for the wallet. I figured I'd better somehow phone home for more money — but gee, the whole thought of it felt terrible. Especially after how careful I'd been about spending.

Just before leaving the place, I took one more look around . . . and found the wallet! It was right where I had idiotically put it — not just under the pillow, but inside the pillow-slip. What a dunce! What a relief!!

9

At this point, memory hasn't left a clue, as to what I did next. I think I spent the next night in Olympia, reclaiming my used-car-lot sleeping quarters that did me good service on the way north — but I honestly cannot say it happened that way. The very next *sure* memory I have is coming into a small town on the coast of Oregon called Yachats, being dropped off practically at the door of a two-story frame hotel painted bright yellow with white trim in a quaint Cape Cod style, right out of a travel brochure — so appealing that I decided to relax my road-weary bones for this night in a real hotel bed, in a private room. It could very well turn out to be my last road night, with a little luck the next day, and I deserved the treat.

It was not my last road night, however. There would be one more, leaving a memory rich enough in detail to outshine everything else on the journey.

Coastal Oregon is one long stretch of magnificent beaches with surf-resistant rocks that stand beyond the sands, roads graced by rhododendrons all the way and dotted with one colorful coastal community after another. A few of them are wide, deep draft harbors, but most only places for fishing boats to congregate, where a stream empties into the surf — every one of them picturesque, whatever the style. I made a good choice, in coming home this way.

Getting close to the California line – maybe about twenty miles distant from it – one of the smallest of these settlements, barely more than a general store and its post office at roadside, was located where the dwindling Pistol River reaches the ocean, and named for it. It hardly qualified as a river, though 'signed' as such at the bridge crossing. I am very clear on it, because I had occasion to remember the driver who let me off there when he reached his home, an isolated frame cottage up a straight-on hillside stairway of perhaps twenty steps. It was directly south of the bridge, on the west side of the highway, and I don't recall any other structures at all, nearby. It would have meant nothing to me, and been as quickly forgotten as the rest, but for the very next driver that gave me a ride.

It was late afternoon by this time; in fact, I think the Pistol River driver had been coming home from a day's work. There wasn't much traffic on the road, and I was never happy standing around waiting for it, without good reason. So I walked on down the road — which was really *up* the road, as it climbed gently toward and into the wooded hills. Maybe fifteen or twenty minutes into this walk, a car came along and stopped for me.

He said he was headed for San Francisco, which was certainly the best thing I could ask. Just what I was hoping for, in fact, all day. So I wasn't inclined to be critical, though I certainly thought it odd, when he made a deal with a service station owner a few miles further along, for a full tank of gas, in trade for what I could see was an expensive set of machine tools. It wasn't that he lacked money for the gas, but he didn't have the required *ration stamps* for it. He said he'd already used up his month's quota — but he didn't seem the least bit remorseful, when we were back underway, about the costly trade he made for it.

He was a lot more relaxed, once we had the gas, and he offered to share some of the food he was nibbling on. It looked like he had just come from a shopping trip, with several bags of groceries, and was eating from whatever he could open, which also seemed a little bit odd.

I wasn't sure what to make of it all, but when we came to the road signs about an agricultural inspection station up ahead at the state line, it began to dawn on me, what was going on. He got nervous again, wondering if I knew anything about the inspection — which I didn't, of course. He asked what I thought they'd do if he just drove on by without stopping for the inspection.

I wanted to tell him it didn't sound like such a good idea. It's always better to bluff your way than show your hand, and you often get away with it. But I still wasn't sure what his problem was, and I didn't want to get involved in it, myself. So I just said, "Hey, I can't give you any advice — it's entirely up to you."

And there went my ride that was going to take me all the way home. The guy just blithely drove on by the inspection station, and almost immediately we heard the sirens behind us.

It turned out that he stole the car, back up the coast in Reedsport. He freely admitted it, and told them that I wasn't in on it, but they held both of us there, anyway, because it was outside California's jurisdiction. We had to wait until an Oregon sheriff came down from Gold Beach, about 35 miles back, which took another couple hours. The only thing I felt good about was that I had taken Dad's advice and left the gun at home.

The Gold Beach sheriff wouldn't take anyone's word for it, either. They had to have proof that I wasn't with this guy when he took the car in Reedsport. So I had to go back with them, and see if I could find that fellow in Pistol River who had given me the previous ride. By sheer, outrageous luck, I knew where he lived.

By the time we got there, after all the paper work and talk between the police from both jurisdictions, and after all the waiting in the first place, it was close to two o'clock in the morning, and they had to roust the poor guy from his sleep, at the house I pointed out. He sleepily identified me as the fellow he'd picked up on the road, all those hours ago.

"Okay," says the Sheriff's deputy, with a big grin, "you're free to go!"

"Wait a minute," says I. "At this hour, on this pitch black road, I don't have anywhere to go. Why don't you just take me back with you and let me spend the rest of the night in your jail?"

So that was how I spent the last night of my great vacation in an Oregon jail. It wasn't much of a night's sleep, but it had the advantage of a blanket and pillow. They let me out at 7 a.m. when they took their prisoner for breakfast, and we sat at opposite counters facing each other as we had our morning's wake-up fare. Him in handcuffs and me free. I don't recall that we had anything to say to each other.

The only other thing of remembered note, as that day took me back home, was a funny moment somewhere south of Fort Bragg, where I was standing in the bright sun, in the hitch-hiker's usual expectant mode, when my eyes met those of a passenger in a passing car, and we exchanged shocked glances of recognition — it was my high school home-room teacher, Mr. Dunn. That 'snapshot' view of him remains, all these years later, though he was gone in an instant. And neither of us ever later spoke of it, for heaven only knows what reason.

Episode 1.2

Before the Time of Smog and Raging Traffic

With 1945 came the end of the war, and even before that the finish of my high school days. Suddenly, I had a world of time to myself with no immediate demands being made of it. No immediate money to speak of, either, except for the pocket cash from part-time work. But spring was in the air, and a regular daily job could wait . . . until I got another good hitch-hike under my travel-hungry belt

The best excuse I could come up with, for a long road trip, was to head for New Mexico and visit my old school buddy, Frank, cooped up in an Air Force training program at Carlsbad Air Base.

I had sense enough, this time, to prepare for the chill nights with a sleeping bag. I found a khaki colored one to match my look-like-GI gear, and it rolled up nicely into a compact 30-inch bedroll, easily handled. I could stuff a wool cap into one end of it, and needed no more luggage than that. I certainly didn't want any pack on my back. A pair of underwear and extra socks fit nicely into my jacket pockets and I could manage a full week without a shower, if necessary — though it never was.

Heading south from San Francisco in those pre-freeway days was no more of a chore than a long and easy walk out Bayshore Blvd. from Potrero, until it felt like time to pause and start thumbing. What little walking I actually had to do was in the bright morning sunlight of a time before San Franciscans ever experienced smog. I have a flash memory of walking along, on that lovely spring morning, with a now-forgotten song from some contemporary movie on my lips – *Califor-ni-ay* – a song that's certainly as remote from the California of today as any reflection on the time before smog, or any thought that it had ever even been that way once.

Somewhere along the way, that first day – probably out of Gilroy – I made the eastward detour over the hills and through the San Joaquin Valley toward Hwy. 99 which figured to get me south quite a bit faster than the short hops on Hwy. 101. Maybe even clear into L.A.

Evening came down, however, before I could even get as far as Bakersfield. I found myself at a highway truck stop, with traffic suddenly dead along the way — or stopped for dinner, who could say? At any rate, it seemed likely I'd get stuck there for the night. I wasn't into night hitching, and I hadn't any awareness of the art of going inside a truck stop and talking-up some driver for a ride. But I had one more idea to try before giving it up for the night.

Hwy. 99 was just a two-lane road, in this section, and the big rigs were parked along the roadside, so there was no problem knowing which way they were headed. There was almost as little problem getting inside one that just had canvas tied down for a back-end closure. It offered just enough space between the edge of the truck bed and its payload container inside, to hold me comfortably. I left some slack when I tied the canvas back down, for visibility, and in less than a half-hour I was again on my way.

Once past Bakersfield, I figured the truck was headed all the way to L.A., but I was wrong. We took a turn to the west, off #99, from somewhere up on the ridge route, the mountainous divide that separates California's Central Valley from the Los Angeles basin. On and on into the night we went, on a less-traveled road — heaven only knew where to, but there was nothing I could do about it. Finally, we pulled off into a small town, a place I'd never heard of called Saticoy, and the driver backed his truck up to the platform of a big lemon cooperative. His payload, I soon found out, was tons of freshly picked lemons, huge containers of them. I scrambled off the truck without being seen by anyone, and found a grassy spot where I could sleep through the rest of the night.

Over a minimalist breakfast, that morning, I reconnoitered the situation. It turned out that I was just a few miles from the coast — I might as well have stayed right on Hwy 101 in the first place. But the map indicated I now had easy access into Santa Monica, and I could pay a visit to Norma, a girl I'd briefly met on a camping trip, the previous year. I hadn't thought about it in my original plan to travel Hwy. 99.

It was a nice diversion from the road trip. I had little trouble finding her, and she was surprised when I turned up on her doorstep. Other than a few letters sent back and forth, there wasn't anything 'going on' between us, so we simply enjoyed the rest of that day together, and I slept out in her yard that night before heading back out on the highway. I really don't remember much of the visit, except that I 'threatened' to kiss her goodbye, and she threatened to whack me if I tried it. So much for my sudden romantic impulses.

Los Angeles had the extensive Pacific Electric Railway system in those days, and I took it for some distance out beyond the immediate suburbs – I don't recall exactly how far – to where I could start hitching again. I definitely recall, though, how lovely it was to walk the open highway, afterwards, leisurely thumbing for my next ride under an incredibly blue southland sky that merely vied for my gratitude with the greens and oranges of endless citrus groves. How it could get any better than that, I still can't imagine.

By nightfall, I was in a truck again – but this time, more circumspectly in the cab of it – heading out of Banning, south of San Bernardino, toward El Centro. I recall the ride mainly for a bit of geographical mis-information the driver imparted: "See the lights over there?" he said, pointing to a dimly visible cluster over the dark Salton Sea. "That's Niland," he added, without my even having to ask. And for years afterward, I was quite sure that there was "an island" in the middle of the Salton Sea.

It was close on midnight by the time he let me off in El Centro, and I was right into my search for some congenial sleeping spot, made the more particular by clouds that threatened rainfall before daybreak. I needed a sheltered place, this time.

I tried the handle, gently, on what seemed an empty, small trailer sitting on a backyard lawn, but came a gruff voice from within: "Who's that?" So I backed off and tiptoed carefully away. Then I found a conveniently ajar window at the rear of a used furniture store. It was a kind of transom window at ground level, that only a slim guy like me could fit through — in fact, I barely made it, dropping down inside to a half basement level, where I found enough old couches to give me all the choice I could ask for. What a gift!

I slept soundly there, and didn't stir until awakened by voices somewhere else in the store. I pulled my stuff together as quietly and quickly as I could. Realizing that I could never make it back out the way I came in, I brazenly walked out the front door of the place. If anyone saw me leave, they were speechless, unable to imagine where I'd come from.

I don't think I've ever gotten used to the daily temperature swing in the high plateau desert country; I was certainly caught off guard by it on this April trip into the southwest, and my cheap sleeping bag was hardly up to the test it was getting. I found I had to sleep in my full clothing, and then take off as much as I could manage as the day progressed.

It took me most of a hot day to make the 60 miles from El Centro to Yuma, and I hung around that town until it cooled a bit before starting to thumb again, late in the day. But by dark, I hadn't even had the hint of a ride. Intending a really early start in the morning, I slept as well as I could, nearby, behind a signboard.

But early did me no good the next day, as it got hotter and hotter and hotter. It almost seemed as though the town delighted in letting hitch-hikers bake. I took it all day, finally realizing at 5 p.m. – after 24 hours in that beastly town – that I had to do something different. Just across the highway was one of the largest rail yards I had come across, and I figured it was time to take my chances with it.

With no way of knowing how to find the train that would get me on my way, from among all the rest on the dozens of tracks, I cautiously approached a decent looking guy working there. I was well aware of the tales of yard-dicks and how they roust hoboes, but there was no point in making a wild guess, or worse yet, trying to grab one on the run. It was the right decision, and he pointed me to a freight that would roll east that night.

What I clambered onto was a flat car with a giant earth-mover securely lashed to it. New and unused, it was part of a military shipment, and I settled on it for the partial shelter of its huge dirt trough, long and wide enough to easily hold my laid out sleeping bag, and deep enough to reasonably assure protection from night winds. Before dark we were underway — onward out of Yuma, hell hole of the west!

I had no idea where to, but I sure didn't have to worry about getting off anytime I wanted to. That freight train hit a high speed of about ten miles per hour. We were all night, and then some – an expectably frigid night – getting to Phoenix. I did the best I could with it. The earth-mover provided nothing in the way of comfort, but did its intended job of keeping me out of the wind. And the heavens that night were something to behold . . . mind-blowing, to a city kid, in their clarity.

As soon as the morning sun came up, I could feel the change. In one more hour, I was dangling my legs from the flatcar as I soaked in the sun's warmth and watched the desert saguaro drift by. At ten miles per hour, it wasn't even like being on a train, more like a Disneyland ride, slowly passing occasional work crews that stood aside for us, waving or nodding as we traded smiles. I wasn't sure if I could be seen from the caboose, or not, but I didn't really care a whole lot by that time.

We got into Phoenix around noon, by which time I'd been checked out by one of the crew who came by while we paused at a water tower, and said it was fine with them if I wanted to ride all the way to Florence Junction, where they'd be switching tracks and cars. So I stayed aboard, even though I was getting hungry. I still had water left, and Florence was just another few hours away. What the heck!

Back on the highway after a very late breakfast, I lucked into a ride going all the way to El Paso. But it was a weird one, I'll tell you. This guy didn't stop for much of anything and it was a really long drive. Today, Hwy 10 zips you practically straight through, from Tucson to Lordsburg and beyond, but in those days the main road was Hwy 80, taking a dip at Benson that twisted through every small town along the way. He wanted me to rub his shoulder most of the time, after it got dark — so he could keep going, he said. When we got to El Paso, he said he had to go across the border into Juarez to get something, and asked if I wanted to go along. Never having been 'abroad', I figured I might as well take him up on it.

He parks his car when we get there, and goes into some fancy establishment, and I go along with him, and he buys a bottle of liquor, which is cheaper there by quite a bit, he says, than in El Paso. While he's getting it, a kind of sexy-looking woman comes down the stairs from a balcony, and asks if we want any girls! She doesn't ask me, she asks my momentary companion, and he says, "No," and turns to me with "How about you?"

Well, I don't quite know what to make of all this, but I figure it's safer to stay clear of it in a Mexican border town, so I turn it down, too. But I'm starting to wonder why *he* turned it down!

He drives us back across the border, and wants to know if I have any place to sleep . . . and by now, I'm more sure of the drift of it all, so I just tell him I think I'd prefer to sleep out in the open air – the cold open air – tonight, and he shrugs his shoulders and says, "Suit yourself."

Off I go, then – and it's after midnight now – to see how I'm going to handle another frigid desert night, and wondering if I might have been a bit hasty about turning down what was clearly moving toward the offer of a warm night's shelter.

I walked out toward the edge of town, which wasn't all that far in those days, along the road I'd be hitching on. When the houses started thinning out, I came to one entirely darkened, with two cars backed into its nearby garage, and the garage door left wide open. *Anything* being better than nothing, at this hour, it seemed a good idea to make use of that open garage, and I laid my sleeping bag out at the very back of it so I wouldn't be seen if anyone came out early and just drove off in one of the cars.

I woke up with the first light, though, and figured I could get up and out of there before anyone would be the wiser. And I nearly made it, but a guy came for his car just as I was tightening my rolled-up sleeping bag, otherwise ready to go. I had no real choice, now, but to walk out past him. I gave him my cheeriest "Good morning!" as I did so, and left him standing there with his mouth hanging open, his breath churning out steam in the cold air, while I headed directly for the road, not fifty feet distant. What could he say?

I wasn't all that impressed with what I saw of Texas, that day, wondering why it had been the object of such childhood fantasies. The movies, of course . . . the American Fantasy Machine had gotten in the way of all the common sense that might have told me what a dry and empty land it really is. California was still the best of all worlds, notwithstanding the tales of 'the West' that I grew up on.

My next stop, and final destination, was Carlsbad Army Air Base, where my old buddy, Frank, was in training. Maybe it had been a year since I'd seen him, maybe less, but we were at an age when friendships shift quickly, for a lot of good and bad reasons — distance certainly among them. Still, there was a genuine enthusiasm mixed with his surprise at seeing me, and I found myself swept into his day's activity more than I could have foreseen. In fact, I provided the occasion for Frank and his service buddies to see what they could collectively pull off, right under the noses of their officers.

For four full days and nights they kept me in their barracks, shifting me from one cot to another as guys came back from

22

or went on leave, making sure I was up and out of there for the morning bed check, getting me fed in the mess hall, and whatever else the occasion required, including GI clothing. It was real sport and fun, and I was into it as much as they were. I think we were all sorry to see it end when the time came for me to leave.

Maybe everything after that was just anti-climactic, I don't know, but memory doesn't favor me with much at all, of the return journey. I came home by way of Albuquerque and Flagstaff, and I recall one more frigid morning in Grants, New Mexico — possibly because I tried cream in my coffee for the very first and very last time. But precious little more of that return journey remains with me.

My head was preoccupied with two of that year's favorite songs, linked in memory with that southwestern road trip . . .

I was taken for a sleigh ride in July.
Oh, I must have been a set up for a sigh...
My dreams were safe all winter,
And then to think that I
Was taken for a sleigh ride in July . . .

Dinah Shore, of course.

The other was written and sung by Johnny Mercer...

...I wish that there were four of her
So I could love much more of her.
She has taken my complete heart,
I've got a sweet tooth for my sweetheart,
Candy, it's gonna be just dandy,
The day I take my Candy,
And make her mine, all mine.

The Square I Became

All it took was twenty years in the world of Employment, Commerce & Getting ahead. With a little patience, anyone can make this transition.

– Interlude –

I had little occasion to hitch-hike after starting college in 1946; and when I got my own car, in 1951, I left it entirely behind — for twenty long years of the struggle and strain of trying to lead a normal, 'respectable' life.

When finally disabused of that notion, in 1971, I got back into hitch-hiking only as an uncomfortable necessity, being now without an automobile or any regular income. The full story of that turnaround will be detailed in a forthcoming autobiography; but pertinent to the immediate writing, I found myself living with a country collective in a Bay Area locale called Canyon, a dozen miles from the nearest public transportation, leaving me with no other alternative than hitch-hiking for getting out to town and back home again.

Fortunately, a hitch-hiking renaissance was underway in those years, to cushion the almost forgotten experience of standing 'nakedly' at the roadside, letting one and all see how 'helpless and vulnerable' I had become. It was an unexpected discovery, in that first year of my return to this once carefree pastime, how much my outlook on it had changed. It meant, of course, how much *I, myself*, had changed, and it gave me considerable pause for reflection on what living in this culture does to a person. I might even say that this reflection greatly influenced the re-shaping of my life, from that point on.

In time, the old carefree feeling returned. It even expanded, to the point where it became an absolutely uplifting venture to just get out on the open road and go somewhere, for the pure fun of it. Over the succeeding years, I lived in such out-of-the-way places (from the central Bay Area) as Sonoma, Carmel, and up at a mountainside camp near Middletown, wherefrom hitch-hiking became my regular commuting mode for visiting the city.

So regular, in fact, that I knew the timing I could rely on, and was seldom more than an hour off the reckoning. As if it were a game of golf, I had a 'par' number of rides that I could keep score by, for each such route,.

In time, too, I gradually became aware of another dimension to this very ordinary and happenstance way of travel. 'Another dimension' in the most profound sense, for it came to seem like whenever I set out on a hitch-hiking journey, I stepped into another reality . . . a world so richly embroidered with coincidence and synchronicities as to challenge the common notion that they are chance events. My rational mind simply couldn't accept them any longer as chance events, for they happened far too often to continue passing it off in those terms.

In the tales that follow, you'll see what I mean.

It was Jung who developed the concept of a synchronicity as an instance of 'meaningful coincidence': a chance happening, in appearance, that yet has a meaningful consequence in the course of one's life, be it on a simple daily basis or in the grander scheme of things. And the everyday, ordinary process of hitch-hiking seems to bring such synchronicities into high profile, with a frequency and regularity that quite persuades one of their meta-rational actuality.

For better or worse, I am characteristically given to rational analysis and not inclined to merely shrug my shoulders at such 'perverse' indications of a world that is other than rational. So this phenomenon has always been a challenge to me, a prod to try and figure out what is really going on.

The best I've been able to come up with, by way of explanation, is that *this is the nature* of actual reality; that we shield ourselves from its mystical implications by exerting as much control over life's process as we can possibly manage, so as to assure ourselves, daily, that we do have determination of our own lives in our own hands, and at a conscious level. The truth of the matter becomes visible, however, in those generally rare moments when control is clearly out of our hands; and hitch-hiking is that notably scarce opportunity for a *willing release* from the almost instinctively driven control effort that shields us from the mystical truth of things.

This, at least, is what I've come to believe. And believing it makes my life not one bit less interesting, productive or secure. In fact, I really do feel that it has enhanced those three qualities beyond measure.

But why am I making a lecture out of it? Read on, and see for yourself.

Great Scott!

Hitch-hiking, in the first few years of my resumption
of it, was mainly local and utilitarian. But in the summer
of 1974, I headed out for Utah. I was trying to redefine a
love affair that hadn't fully knit into a solid relationship.
Roberta and I spent a brief summer together in Sonoma,
but we couldn't make a go of it, so she had gone on with
her kids to Moab, her onetime family home. I was intent
on salvaging a friendship from the busted romance when I
took off for that visit, and might never have written about
it had not the journey, itself, produced some memorable
moments worthy of a tale. I wrote it for a more immediate
readership in a Black Bart newsletter.

I set out for Utah early in May – hitch-hiking, of course – with fifty dollars in my pocket and another fifty hanging back in my checking account. What little more I had, in my insolvent way, was left beyond reach until my return. What I took should suffice for a 3 or 4-week visit with Roberta, a thousand miles from home.

It would be the longest hitching trip yet, in my new alternative life. Two years ago I hitched up to Oregon, but I have learned a good deal about hitch-hiking since then, and about life itself, and I pretty well knew it was likely to be a different sort of experience — but could hardly have foreseen what actually took place.

I had always thought of hitch-hiking as a very unique and challenging method for getting from one place to another — with undercurrents of excitement as well as exasperation, and much reality-testing of one kind and another, but essentially a means of transport. Now I was moving toward a complete reversal of that view. Hitch-hiking is a situational stage for karmic expression and discovery. 'Getting there' is simply an excuse for the opportunity to go below our cultural facade and come face-to-face with the realities of living.

Looked at in that way, it compares in some respects with relationships and job situations, which are probably the major situational stages in our lives. It does not have the deep intensity of a relationship or the purposeful seriousness of a job, nor the long-term involvement of either one of those. But in exchange, it is relatively free of the heavy encrustation of ethical illusion that surrounds work and relationship situations. We can observe the interflow of one event with another, and their effects on our own feelings, without such monumental veils as Love and Responsibility and Maturity coming in to distort the view and defeat the message.

But I had to be somewhat free of those veils in the whole arena of living before I could really see the beautiful karmic expression of life, as it takes place on the road. This trip became an unbelievable karmic package for me, neatly boxed and tied with a ribbon by someone (or perhaps some force?) I came to know as Scott.

I started at high noon on a Friday from Berkeley's University Avenue, a prime take-off point for nearly anywhere, for it links to all major routes. Usually stacked with travelers [in the 1970s] along its traffic-heavy length, the wait could be long — but it's all up for grabs in this very unique reality, and the experienced hitch-hiker takes his (or her) place, anywhere along the half-mile stretch of Avenue, with as little hope or expectation as possible.

I waited an hour, calm and relaxed; two hours, getting fidgety but not nervous; took time out for some coffee and toast to break the monotony; three hours, and seriously beginning to wonder if I'd get out of the bay area that night. I was worried that I might get a short ride to a worse location, and even concerned, now, about the most likely long ride, which would put me in the maelstrom of Sacramento, about 80 miles away, from where it's very difficult to find a good departure spot in the late hours of the day. A car finally pulled up a little after 3 p.m. and I edgily asked how far he was going.

"Reno," he replied, and that was all it took.

In one quick instant, the whole day and my whole sense of it had been reversed. I was high on that, of course, but the lesson of it was not lost on me: the next minute is *always* fresh and new, with all the possibilities of the very first minute. Feelings, fears, and all the concerns about what you are doing right or wrong have no relevance at all to what is happening or about to happen. The ride was a good omen for the whole trip, and I settled back to enjoy the three-hour cruise, the good conversation, and some of the most mellowing grass I've ever been privileged to have shared with me.

In Reno, the light of day was just starting to fade. A short, quick ride took me to the far edge of town, and I found an isolated and hidden spot behind a roadstop drinking house that seemed to be ignored by all the passing cars. The stars were bright, the noise was easy, and I had a grand sleep right through to daybreak.

I was practically on top of a freeway ramp, and there I encountered a young fellow also heading out across the wide expanse of western desert. He was going to Colorado. I don't ordinarily join up with other hitchers, but the local police made it easy for us, and almost mandatory. We had to relocate, we were told, to a spot about a mile up the freeway where the jurisdictions of city and county touch. All of the regional police had agreed that it was easier to expel unwanted, often penniless strays from that easy exit point, than to have them wandering the freeway accesses from one end of town to the other, in that highly respectable community known as Reno.

Scott Cressey was my friend's name, and the two of us got to know each other as we plodded the early morning mile along the freeway, and thumbed from our assigned spot. Scott had all sorts of tales about the awful desert ahead of us, and how thoroughly inhospitable were the various one-horse constabularies along the way. Anything between here and Salt Lake City would be a deadfall, he warned, and so we agreed to stand firm until we got that long ride, for there was not possibly a better place anywhere to get it from. We were in range of vision from the full freeway, and it was so early that we had no competition.

So we waited. In comfort, in company, and in absolutely good spirits. One hour. Someone pulled over and offered to take us 40 miles further into Nevada, and we graciously declined. Two hours. Someone was going 25 down the line. Thanks, but no thanks. Three hours (really, it was like clockwork). Someone said 15 miles? Scott and I looked at each other, but we held firm and waved them on.

That's when it dried up. We waited … hour on hour, as the sun reached and went on by its zenith. Our talking lagged, and the heat of the day was beginning to get to us. Finally, I started questioning this whole thing; something was there that I was not looking at. I was willing to accept the longer wait for the more selective ride, but some other message was trying to come through here, with the situation of diminishing offers right from the very start of it.

Of course! It was a matter of distance and greed, not just waiting for the right ride. I had long since learned not to be greedy about money, and here I was being greedy about miles! I talked this over with Scott, and we agreed to take the next ride, *wherever* it might take us. And I was quite sure it would be the shortest offer of all.

Sure enough — within a half hour, a little old fellow in a pickup truck offered to take us ten miles out into the desert. No hesitation at all — we grabbed it. It was the right ride for this situation, as all the others had been, and we had no regrets after spending seven hours in one place to learn the lesson. He let us out at an isolated crossroads café, turning off onto a dusty side road, himself. We ate, and then took ourselves up the road a bit, to await whatever might transpire. It was 3:30 in the afternoon, and we had progressed all of ten miles.

Within another half hour, Scott and I were in a car going clear through to Salt Lake City, for me, and on beyond for him. It was so instructively precise that I could hardly believe it, for we never would have gotten the ride from our Reno outpost. These folks recalled passing some hitch-hikers at that very spot, unable to stop for them because a police car was sitting nearby, watching the freeway traffic, almost daring any driver to pull over and risk a citation.

The ride was continuous and uneventful, except that I contributed five dollars of my narrow funds for gas, to see them through their journey. Well after midnight, at a freeway junction on the outskirts of Salt Lake City, I said good-byes and found myself a grassy spot to lay out my sleeping bag for the remaining hours of darkness.

Sunday was a wild one — I still had some lessons to learn. Most of the morning was spent wandering from one freeway access to another, seeking the 'right' one — always a problem for me in a strange city. I finally got a ride carrying me about 50 miles closer to my goal, but it left me at a rather odd place with a choice of another ten-mile freeway hop to the junction I really wanted, or some equally uninviting town-hopping on secondary roads. On the one hand, cars were very inhospitably zipping along, with almost nothing going into the stream at this point, and on the other was the prospect of about 3 or 4 tiny rides, through as many tiny communities, and possibly as many hours, for that is the nature of secondary rural roads. I walked over to a service station to get a good look at a good map and verify all my indecisions.

Then a shining bit of wisdom hit me, and I said to myself: here is where I am, and here is where I proceed from; and right outside the service station, I 'proceeded' down along the secondary route. That is to say, my thumb proceeded, while I sat comfortably on a roadside bulkhead and enjoyed the scenery.

After a few dozen cars had gone by, along came a hot rod, driven by a young hotshot — an absolutely unstoppable combination. Sure enough, he zoomed by me, and then – as though *he'd* been struck by a beam of wisdom – he screeched to a stop. Wherever I wanted to go, he said. He was just joy-riding, and within reason it didn't make any difference where.

You'd better believe that things like that are karmic. He took me all the way through the small towns and secondary road switches, right to the threshold of my last open highway run. It was like a divine reply, to validate my discovery of the here-and-now. And from that point, I was 'home free' with a quickly obtained ride in the back of a pickup, and open-air desert scenery all the way into Moab.

Desert mini-metropolis, all of about a mile square, surrounded by open, red-canyon country and the Colorado River: a green-bordered touch of refreshment right outside of town, Moab was a spring-blossoming oasis, filled with small-town children and short-haired oldsters, rock shops and river tours.

I had a warm surprise awaiting me. Roberta had gone on a weekend river trip – an opportunity no one in their right mind would turn down – but had let it be known that I might arrive that weekend. That is, to her community action group who were helping to put on a festival, that weekend, in the town square. I strolled into the midst of it, like any wandering hobo, with my bedroll over my shoulder. A totally strange blond woman came over and asked if I was Irv Thomas — a thousand miles from where anyone even knew me! That was Lucia, Roberta's closest cohort, and before I knew it I was practically surrounded by young people, and in a matter of hours I felt like a part of the community.

When Roberta got home, I felt the sparks of her personality all over the place; same old Roberta, same old feelings, and same old house full of more people than I could ever keep track of. For a brief while, it felt like I was home. The summer before, we had tried a relationship in Sonoma, but the separate pull in each of our lives – hers toward family and mine toward writing – kept it from jelling. We wanted to hang onto the friendship, though, and this was our first real try at it.

The edges of this new kind of relationship were a bit rough for me; I had to feel my way through it, with very little sureness of what was right and what was not. I wanted to feel and express my closeness to her, as before, but I knew there had to be limits. I had to discover where they were, yet I had no taste for the awkwardness of discussing it. But it was mellow and it was good. At least for the first part of my stay.

By the second week, I found something to start hassling myself about, much as I had vowed to stay off that deadly trip.

35

By good or poor fortune – I wasn't yet sure – I had come to Moab at the very moment of the year when Roberta was about to get involved in a new relationship. She didn't know that when I arrived, any more than I did. But by the time I was ready to return to California, it was pretty apparent to both of us, all of us.

Scott was his name, strangely enough. Scott Smith. I had met him that day in the park, and I liked him instantly. He was a quiet, deep person close to Roberta's more youthful age, much into naturalism, his own music, and a very soul-oriented way of living. I could not help but like him. That made it easier, but I was not yet free enough of Roberta – in my own head – for it to be that easy.

And I had to look at that, first of all. I had not come to Utah to reconstitute anything with Roberta, and I had fully anticipated the possibility that she might be close to someone else. But seeing it happen was exposing the real level of my feelings, and they were an odd blend. I really liked Scott, and I really wanted to feel supportive of their closeness. But it was a lonely sensation to watch the two of them together. I found my whole response to Scott being affected by it. And I found that I was less and less able to feel openly expressive with Roberta. I was going through a microcosm of the struggle in Sonoma.

Fortunately, it was at a much reduced level. I could tell myself that it was good for me, because I needed it to shake out all the hidden feelings that I hadn't yet come to grips with in the process of constructing my new Roberta reality. And what about that new reality! Was it going to be a real one, or not?

One technique – one statement to myself, repeated over and over, as often as I found myself becoming uptight – helped more than anything else did. I simply said to myself, "I am not here in

Moab to achieve or accomplish anything at all." It worked well enough to keep my head clear for the rest of my stay.

In retrospect, I think it was a very beautiful and fortuitous experience, to have been their while Roberta's love for Scott took shape. The fact that it was a bit hard for me to handle makes it all the more so. In its own way, it contributed to my growth, and to the growing bond between Roberta and me, because the ultimate reflection and correspondence about it substantiated once and for all that our bond stood firmly and strongly beyond the limited range of our emotional experience with each other. And perhaps that is what I had really gone to Utah to find out.

The trip home was a good deal more than anti-climax. It rounded out the karmic package or the whole experience in an absolutely perfect sequence of events. I rode with Roberta to Salt Lake City, for a visit with her brothers timed with my departure. The younger of them, Robert, drove me out to the far end of town early the following morning. And from there, I got a fairly quick ride out to the jump-off point on the Utah side of the great Nevada desert — the very last and biggest truckstop on the edge of a vast emptiness. Here it was that the great and final test of my acceptance of all things was to take place.

As we reached the truckstop, I counted at least eight people spaced along the highway, thumbing for westward rides. It'll be a long wait, I told myself, and I might as well get fortified with coffee and toast. When I emerged from the truckstop, all the other hitchers were gone. It could only have been one of those rare drivers who pick up everyone in sight — and I had opted, unknowingly, for coffee and toast instead.

I smelled something karmic right then and there. It didn't make any difference at all, what had happened to those other road people, or why I hadn't been among them; here I was, and this was right where I was at!

37

It was, indeed, a long wait. Hour after hour after hour, through afternoon and into evening. I knew it was going to be a long wait, and my spirits did not sag for one moment; nor was I into any headtrips with each approaching and passing car. I just enjoyed it all, until the setting sun made it too cold to stand there any longer. Then I had a warm bite of food and a good night's sleep out in the nearby tall grass. When I awoke, there was frost all along the top surface of my sleeping bag. A hot breakfast took the chill off both me and the morning, and I was out there once again, in all the zest of a fresh new day, knowing that sooner or later my ride would come.

I was being put through a rigorous test of acceptance, and I honestly felt that the ride would not come till late that day. I felt, too, that the ride would be a long one to compensate me for the struggle — which was no struggle at all. During that morning, out on the road, I had an absolutely beautiful flash insight about the whole traveling experience — Roberta and all of it. I could not be greedy about money, I could not be greedy about miles or rides, and I could not be greedy about closeness with people; all things come in their own time, and are not mine to keep or covet — just to enjoy and learn from. It is, indeed, a very beautiful world. And I thought about the strange fact that a man named Scott had been connected with both significant parts of my karmic trip. What an odd coincidence.

Sometime before noon, much to my surprise, a little zippy sportscar, driven by a zippy young blond fellow, pulled over and stopped for me. It had been seven road hours for me — the same number, I later realized, that I had spent with Scott outside of Reno.

"San Francisco!" He said it with exuberance, as though he expected some kind of joyous whoop out of me.

"You're early!" was all I could manage to come up with. And off we zipped, out into the Utah-Nevada desert, while I did my best to explain to him the reason for my foolish and impertinent answer. To no avail — he did not even seem to know what karma meant.

It made no difference, anyhow. We would find many other things to talk about, on the long ride home.

"By the way, my name's Irv," I said. 'What's yours?"

"Scott," he said, with a wide and strangely meaningful grin. "Scott Dahl."

"Oh.   Sure ... naturally." I just shook my head in utter, amazed disbelief, knowing full well that no one would ever believe this story. But – so...help...me, Scott – it really happened.

Tript-hytch (1978-81)

*I've tried to find the earliest things I've written, about
this regained mode of travel in my life, hoping to catch
the reflection of my dawning wonderment at the 'magic'
that ultimately became an almost routine part of the hitch-
hiking experience for me.*

*Some of it is too fragmentary to make a decent tale,
or too interwoven with other material to tell a very clear
story. But I've pegged a few that can be clustered within a
fairly narrow time-frame, maintaining the book's sequence
arrangement.*

*The first of these, and the shortest tale in the book, is
a marvelously linked chain of events that took place on a
return from the Bay Area to Carmel, where I was living
in the spring of 1978.*

*Next is a tale that tells how the road trip began to
blend with what was happening in my world, and shows
how hitch-hiking the road subtly moves toward a hitch-
hiking way of life. This was my report – an earlier version
of which appeared in a Fall 1980 issue of Black Bart
– of a chain of events I came to believe were initiated by
my mother's approaching death, though that awareness
came only after the journey's full development. In point
of immediate awareness, I could only trace it to one of the
most astounding synchronicities of my life — which is
saying a lot, since my life has been filled with them.*

Just try to imagine yourself paying a surprise visit to someone clear across the country. You've never been there before, and are not expected; you've arrived only by the grace of a chance ride offering the evening before, and you can recall telling no one where you'd be going, since you weren't even sure, yourself. Yet, hardly five minutes after your arrival, the friend's phone rings . . . and it's for you!

The third tale of this trio is another shortie which was originally the tail end of a discourse in a 1982 issue of Black Bart *on the wiles and tyranny of an overactive ego, and how it so often has been my own demon, pushing me into the passion of writing in order to 'get published,' when I very well know the destructive effect of that on my creative independence and my sense of well-being. I've long felt that a writer submitting to that passion cannot help but find himself bent – and ultimately bending – to the dictates of the marketplace.*

The tale centers on one such personal bout with my upstart ambition the previous summer, and how the awareness unfolded for me.

The Universe Whole

Now and again, but indeed rarely, a chance occurrence permits us to experience the Universe whole. Seldom is it more than a momentary view; but one to be treasured, even if – especially if – it appears in the mundane.

It happened on a St. Patrick's Day of another year, a crisp and early morning that found me somewhere near midtown San Jose, thumbing for a ride toward the Monterey coast. Perhaps because it was this special morning, two rather unusual things occurred, each involving an exchange of money.

The opener might have been the cost of a ticket to Hermann Hesse's mystical 'magic theater': a somewhat unsteady fellow of my own middling years wanting, at first, to bum a cigarette. Failing in this (because I'm not a smoker), he nervously and very apologetically asked if I could spare the change to buy a pack. I hesitated; I carry very little cash when on the road. But he seemed so absolutely ashamed at being 'reduced to begging' that I finally couldn't refuse him. I paid the price of admission.

Not many minutes later, a more jolly but equally tipsy old-timer, observing me humbly begging for rides, offered me a dollar bill "for a sandwich down the road." I traded him a grateful smile, and accepted. I never reject what the Universe brings. He leaned on his way, but then turned back once more. It seemed to strike him that a dollar no longer buys much of a sandwich.

"Here," he said. "Better take another."

Quite content that I'd been well rewarded for the bread earlier cast upon the water, I thought little more of it until some two hours later, halfway to Monterey. I was in mid-countryside, soaking up the warm sun, waiting as usual for another ride, when a small, not too battered VW pulled up alongside me and a rather worried but hopeful young face peered out.

Would I pay for some gas in exchange for a ride?

This couple, it seems, traveling from Portland to Los Angeles, had camped in a cow pasture somewhere north of San Francisco and had somehow lost a wallet and all their funds on that spring-green hillside. It was realized only as they ordered breakfast in the city. They had no idea where the night was spent, not a single friend in San Francisco on whom to lean, in this emergency, and were caught with nary enough gas either to get where they were going or return whence they came.

It was clearly a desperate situation, and I was clearly in possession of two spare dollars for which they had far more need than I. And I was suddenly gifted with this beautiful view of a Universe in which all things interconnect in some grand and purposeful scheme, of which we seldom see more than our tiny myopic portion.

Episode 3.2

The Phone Call

On a slightly muggy mid-July afternoon in 1980, in New York for my first time in years, I made my way rather uncertainly around upturned cardboard boxes to the poorly lit second floor of a lower west side walk-up, to the dim outline of a door, and knocked several times. The fellow who answered looked only slightly familiar to me — and I, hardly at all to him, for I had grown a beard since the once we had met, five years earlier.

What's more, he was not expecting me. I was three thousand miles from home and I had not written that I'd be visiting. In fact, only the day before had I realized that I could do it. I had been whiling my time in Washington, DC, until Dick Wakefield, my host there, was ready to head for Toronto with me, to take part in a World Futurist Conference. Dick was the one who had set my travels in motion way back in February, and determined its timing as well.

Scott Lewis, who occupied this upstairs flat, was one of only two people that I knew well enough to call on in New York.

He was a correspondent of many years, known through earlier connections though we had only met that one time before, when he was traveling in California. This unannounced return visit had only materialized in the good fortune of finding someone on a University of Georgetown rideboard looking for company on his quick two-day ride home to Jersey City. I'd be on my own until the time came for his Georgetown return.

Scott and I traded the usual amenities of old friends from far places and sat down in his cluttered living room to catch each other up. Not ten minutes into that process, his telephone rang. He went into the adjoining room for it, and I heard only the briefest words before he returned with the phone in his hands and said it was for me!

This, of course, was utterly impossible. "What do you mean?"

"It's for you — here, take it," and he thrust the phone toward me.

He assumed, I suppose, that I had left his number with someone. But I knew I hadn't. I had told Dick only that I had a couple friends in New York to look up, without saying who. I hadn't even been carrying Scott's phone number with me.

I took the phone and inquired rather hesitantly – almost fearfully at this weird manifestation – "Yes...?"

"Is this Irv?" It was a woman's voice.

"Yes?"

"This is JoAnne!"

Then it all flooded in. I *had* written to JoAnne recently, but before knowing I'd be in New York. In fact, my note could have hardly yet made it over to France.

Many months back, when she was planning her return to the States, I wrote that I could conceivably be on the east coast in early July and I did send her Scott's phone number as one place to leave a message for me, or pick one up. And in my usual way, I had then forgotten about it. But it was still virtually impossible that she should pinpoint the very hour of my arrival here, for this was *two weeks beyond* the July 1st estimate that I gave her at that time.

Her flight from France had landed at La Guardia just a few hours before she called, and this exquisitely unplanned coordination between us seemed only to confirm intimations I already had about this journey, almost from its start.

That would be in early February, when Dick had called me from his Bethesda home to ask if I'd be willing to join him at a Futurist Conference in Toronto and make a presentation there, as part of a track on Social and Institutional Change that he was coordinating. To me, at that moment, it was merely putting another plug into the fantasy itinerary that I am always setting up during a dreary winter. What I didn't tell Dick was that invariably, before spring reaches fullness, the *real* agenda for the year's midcourse comes flying at me from some starboard direction, completely wiping out my winter fantasies.

One of the fascinating aspects of living a more natural life is that you never really know what you'll be doing, where you're going to be, from one year to the next. It seems to unfold with a logic of its own, to be discovered as it happens. You end up doing all the right things — but often as not, for all the wrong reasons.

As it happened this year, I *was* to travel; and it was precisely Dick's Toronto invitation that would capture me and hold me on course. However, the true target of the journey, the inner target, was not Toronto but St. Paul — although I didn't even suspect it until I arrived there. I did have a strong sense that the journey was being made for other reasons; that the conference was my carrot-on-a-stick. But nothing else penetrated the screen, even though – as I now see – there were clues scattered all around. But they were too much a part of 'the swirl of real life' to be seen for any deeper content. Only in retrospect, as in the second reading of a mystery, does the screen become transparent.

It wasn't strange enough to flag me, for example, that I wanted to be in Britt, Iowa – just 125 miles from St. Paul – to check out the early-August gathering of hoboes held there each year. Nor the coincidental fact that a west coast friend was to be vacationing in Minnesota at just about the same time. Two good reasons for routing myself in that direction immediately after the conference, and yet they sparked not even a curious flash in this head that has grown used to such signals.

Even more potent, but offering no apparent connection, was the fact that my 78-year-old mother had suffered an immobilizing stroke on the 7th of December. It was the very same day I had been composing a *Black Bart* newsletter ("…I write these very words on December 7th, the anniversary of another day, long ago…") which happened to be the spark for Dick's February inspiration to get in touch with me. But that's a pretty far-fetched string of linkage, isn't it?

Not until the very last day of June did I actually begin the journey. By which time I felt too crowded to hitch-hike, for we had to be in Toronto before July 20, and I wanted to meet Dick in Bethesda a good week earlier. The conference date, once a lightly regarded flip to an imaginary itinerary, had become the cornerstone around which all else revolved.

I managed to turn up a drive-away vehicle; a fine stroke of Providence because the southern route I wanted to travel was already undergoing one of the century's most intolerable heat waves.

I planned on visiting several people along the route, ever hopeful of reclaiming wintertime's fantasy journey. But a strange situation began to develop. In one town after another, the folks that I wanted most to see were not at home. It was almost as if the Universe mocked my petty purposes of travel; or guaranteed, at least, that I wouldn't be side-tracked by them. And the vehicle, of course – its comfortable and speedy consolation – made the bitter pill bearable as it carried me onward.

The journey offered its special rewards nevertheless: sleeping stark naked right out on the prairie, at a discreet distance from El Paso, through midnight sprinkles of a rain that quickly dried; dipping in the warm gulf waters after a night's sleep on a Galveston beach, and seeing both moon and sun rise out of the sea there; picking up a hitch-hiker in Austin and learning that his name was Scott!

I took a two-day breather in New Orleans – the only time I've ever been there – and enjoyed the *Preservation Hall Jazz Band* in its own funky setting. Then I was off on the last leg of the driving journey, to Atlanta, where I delivered the car and picked up a hundred dollars for my trouble, which just about paid my costs up to that point. I was finally back to my more familiar mode of travel: hitch-hiking, and its usual gifts.

It took all afternoon and four rides to get 30 miles out of Atlanta; but then, at about 6 p.m., the long one came along — all the way to Washington, DC. And it was an adventure entirely unto itself.

I was picked up by a black Marine Corps non-com, not in uniform — a fellow tall enough to have been a basketball pro, and a really nice guy. It was an all-night drive, and I guess he wanted the conversation to keep him awake. But I think I was there with him for a whole other reason.

Knowing that anything could happen on a cross-country drive, I had borrowed an AAA card, to have along with me if it should come in handy. I had it with me when the Marine's

49

car lost its engine power somewhere in South Carolina, in the middle of a pitch black night. He had no AAA card of his own, and it was not a good situation for any black person, regardless of all the laws in place. There was no traffic at all, along the road, just a few building lights in the near distance. I figured it was up to me to check them out, and so I did.

One of the buildings had a night watchman who let me use the phone, and I found the nearest all-night AAA response number. In an hour or so, a truck was out there for us, and when its driver found out that we needed a part he didn't have on hand, he graciously took us back home with him, where we spent the rest of the night.

There were no further obstacles. I was in Bethesda the following night, in good time for Dick's expectations. He had a letter from JoAnne for me – for I'd given her his address, too – advising me that she'd surely like my company on her ride back to California from upstate New York, where her old van was in storage. She'd be flying soon, and so I wrote back at once, telling her how to find me *in Toronto,* and suggesting we could ride together from there. And then I put it entirely out of my head. It was three days later that I found my Georgetown ride into New York City, and you know what happened after that.

It was abundantly clear to me, after all this had taken place, that JoAnne had some significant part to play in whatever the real purpose of my journey was all about. A tantalizing thought, but not the least bit informative. I had never known JoAnne on a relationship basis, but one can't stop the inclination to fantasy when something like this is happening.

We joined forces in Toronto just as the conference ended, and prepared to set out westward without delay. Her truck-van seemed in fine spirits, and no problem was in prospect. I travel with a pared-down version of a favorite resource of mine, the *I*

Ching, and I wanted some sort of guideline as to what I might expect of this joined journey back toward home, so I put the question to it: "What is to be my connection with JoAnne?" The response I received was *The Arousing*, moving to *Return* (also called *The Turning Point*).

Now, *The Arousing* is not to be taken in its colloquial western sense. Other translations have rendered it as *Thunder* and *Shocking*. It most simply means 'brace yourself for the unexpected'. A single moving-line added the further cryptic but very evocative detail that "shock is mired...movement is crippled." The idea of *Return* might well relate to the fact that this was a return journey. But if read with the wider implication of *The Turning Point*, it could reference something more significant and open-ended — who knows what? All that seemed fairly clear to me was that the journey's major development lay still ahead.

Before we were even out of Canada the truck developed engine trouble. It got worse in Michigan and impossible by the time we reached Chicago. We found out that a malfunctioning set of lifters had to be replaced, a major repair. A Chicago friend of JoAnne provided shelter for the three days it took, but then she learned that her credit card was not negotiable there. I had no credit card myself, in those days, and almost no funds of my own, so JoAnne had to pay it with cash, which amounted to half of her trip funds. It looked like we'd have to rely on the credit card for gas along the way. I considered that Chicago must be our 'mired in' spot, unable to imagine how it could get any worse.

We leisured up through Wisconsin and into Minnesota, visiting with friends of mine along the way, and finally struck for Minnesota. At this point, there was one remaining night until the hobo gathering, and I still had hopes of making it. From there, we'd proceed straight west to Moscow, Idaho, where JoAnne's brother lived (her own contributing reason for choosing this route). I had two good friends in Minneapolis, either one of whom might offer a night's lodging and some welcome fellowship before we headed for wide open territory. It all looked good.

Until JoAnne discovered that she had lost her credit card. We thought about that, and soberly realized that between the two of us, we hadn't the gas money to reach the coast. Not even Idaho. And that this had to be the last big city we'd see for at least 1500 miles. Suddenly, our whole world had turned from green to red. The only sensible thing to do was plant ourselves right here in Minneapolis and earn the bucks necessary to finish the trip.

JoAnne had her bed-on-wheels, but I'd have to scramble for mine. The folks I knew, there, were not up for anything more than a brief visit. Circumstances are sometimes the only cues we have, so I headed for the twin city, St. Paul, where I could tap into another resource: something called the *Travelers Directory*, which listed two possible St. Paul hosts. Though on different streets, it turned out they were within a block from each other, where the two streets intersected — an odd circumstance that might have said to me (as in 'X' marks the spot) *"here you are!"* but I was too absorbed in the process of living it to see the light go on.

Even more curiously, celebrations were underway at both places when I got there to check them out: a birthday at one and a wedding at the other, and I was suddenly swept into a continuing social round that was to last for several days. And yes, one of them gratifyingly offered lodging — for a full week, as it eventuated. The festive dinners and some superb gospel performances in the first few days of that social whirl kind of lulled me into a well-cared-for neutral zone. I managed to help

JoAnne, along the way of it, with a floor polishing venture, until at long last the fact of *where I was,* and its meaning, finally surfaced in my consciousness.

Not until then did it cross my mind that this was the city my folks had grown up in, married and had their first child (my sister). It wasn't that I had forgotten it, I just hadn't *remembered* it! I had never been to this city before in my 53 years, and the two images of St. Paul were simply in separate compartments: a place on our journey, and the city of my mother's youth. With the recognition, I suddenly found myself wanting to explore — to learn what I could of her old neighborhoods, and find out what traces were still there.

Of our remaining week in St. Paul, then, I put quite a bit of time into it: old records, museums, city directories, half-legible maps and photo repositories of St. Paul's past; I looked into birth and death archives, found the very streets where it all took place . . . bathing myself in my own family history . . . touching that part of my roots I had never known.

We finally made it back to the west coast, of course, and I could hardly wait to go see my mother once again. There was no apparent change in her condition: drawn-in and emaciated features (she was fed by tubes), eyes closed, unresponsive to touch, immobile. I despaired of any hope of communicating. But I sat down and took her hand in mine and began to talk to her.

I told her of my journey to the city where she had grown up, and of how I had found the house next door to the one she would have remembered from childhood – her own was gone – and talked to the people there, old-timers who told me they actually remembered the family! And what the streets were like now, and all the old records I had turned up, and even a pair of cousins I had found — nephews of my long-dead dad. I talked to her for nearly an hour, intent only on recalling as much as I could, and then received a quite unexpected reward: the trace of a tear, welling in the corner of her left eye!

Not many weeks later she died. And I have always suspected that she was only waiting for my return. That perhaps, in fact, she had somehow 'sent me' on that journey, through the strange 'conspiracy' that eventuated between Dick and Scott and JoAnne, along with her miserably upstart and undependable van.

Episode 3.3

A Case of Mistaken Identity

L ast summer I had fairly well talked myself into one of those creative efforts that 'might be good for the world'. It was a book (of course) about my ten years of wandering the wilderness (of course), and I had done about 5000 words of this self-exaltation that I felt fairly good with — in fact, quite invested in. Then a relatively minor question arose about locating a publisher; it brought up another question best settled with the *I Ching* — but this, instead, opened yet another question, and before I knew it, I'd brought down my whole house of confidence in what I was doing. It was a classic case of getting tangled up in my own feet — one value being crossed up by another.

In this instance it was my faith in the *I Ching* versus my sureness that I was on a good writing track. You have to understand, here, that the *I Ching* has seen me through more desperate passages in the last decade of wilderness travel than I care to recall, so that I've come to trust it implicitly in matters at all problematical. It is especially effective when one is lost in the toils of ego.

Very discouraged, and more than a little bitter about the insistent barrier that seems to stand between me and my dreams of glory, I broke loose from the now pointless labor of writing to hitch-hike out toward the coast. I wanted some fresh, cool air and some larger understanding. It had been a well-conceived idea, I was sure; and what if it did involve some ego-tripping? What is so terribly awful about that?

Near the coast, I happened into a not-so-usual hitch-hiking experience: my thumb was ignored by a sight-seeing couple who passed me by, but then doubled back to pick me up. Their reason for returning: they thought I might be the poet, Lawrence Ferlinghetti! Now, I've never met LF, but my instant reaction was that he would never have been out there along the road, either walking or hitching.

I love the way a logjam breaks, letting loose a chain reaction of insights that come tumbling forth in a veritable cascade. My whole world of hitch-hiking began to spin out in a profusion of images: the lovely spring mornings when I literally sing to the passing cars, the many things to be observed at a walker's pace, the sheer sense of adventure in the air, the occasional real stimulation of a stranger's conversation, the meaningful encounters, the excitement of watching another reality take me from point to point to exactly where I'm going, and the usual impossible ride that comes along in any 'impossible' situation. Aside from providing my transportation, hitch-hiking is a pastime that feels singularly 'me', and represents a way of life that I would trade for nothing at all. And in this moment of revelation, I knew that I loved my life, wanted nothing more from it than I already have — not starhood, not name in lights, not anything at all that might threaten this free and easy existence of mine.

It is arguable, certainly, whether I actually risk ever becoming a 'star', and whether – even granting that fantasy – it would keep me from hitch-hiking or anything else. But what must be perfectly evident, and was to me in that mid-August moment of clarity, is that the ego-driven passion overlays all common sense, all reality, all other values, and makes of its victim a Pavlovian pup. Is that really a reason for writing a book? Is it a framework within which to be making serious life-moves?

And yet, I am not cured of the passion. I don't expect I ever will be, because it seems to come with the territory: writing requires readers, even if they only dwell in the anticipations of a tempered imagination; they are always there in prospect. But I learn to treat this 'writer's curse' with a little more thoughtful caution. One good piece of advice recently received was that I may simply not yet be ready to write a book. One so easily ignores the fact that creativity, just like any living thing, needs to ripen — and who is so omniscient as to know when that will have occurred?

Another guideline may lie in a proper respect for the temporality of one's being. A book, if it is to have any vitality at all, must be as much an exploration as an accounting. When it becomes strictly a tale of where one has been, what one has already lived through – especially if it is a tale already told many times and 'frozen' in one's perspective – it can't possibly be anything more than an ego-trip.

On the other hand, a continually told tale can be a constantly evolving statement if it passes through fresh filters of perspective. Whitman wrote his *Leaves of Grass* over and over again, publishing nine different versions in the course of nearly 40 years. And I daresay that *Black Bart* has been doing much the same, in its quarter-term life-span (I doubt that we'll make the full 40. But who knows?).

When I came to the end of these musings that were prompted by a case of mistaken identity on that August day, I found myself unusually content with this peripatetic journal that has, indeed, been my 'Leaves of Grass' these ten long years. In contrast to the many times I have secretly wondered if there would ever be another issue, I knew that in one form or another* it would never end. It is as much a part of my being as the hitch-hiking.

Someday, perhaps, I shall try to catalog all the things that *Black Bart* has been for me. But on the note of this present discussion, I'll only say that it has been my trustworthy guide through the wilds of ego. It has allowed me to believe that I am, indeed, leaving a testament to this world, while at the same time slowly taming that passion; as if letting out a kite on a string, or a fish on a line — allowing the necessary room to run, but slowly, slowly drawing it back to its proper limits.

It may never be much of a testament, residing as it does on poorly grained paper that will stand no test of time, unbound, frail victim to the easiest of accidents . . . but then it is no more frail than I, myself; we are living things, *Black Bart* and I, and the price of life is frailty. Thoughts are frail, so is consciousness, and even love. It may well be that the very best of life can only be found in fleeting transience, and we are just too blind to see it.

---

* *It's interesting, for me, to read those words close to a quarter-century after they were written. Black Bart only lasted a few more years, with occasional newsletters picking up where it left off, for a few more, and then* Ripening Seasons *took up the task a few years after that, for a total continuity (if irregular) of 33 years, so far – of journaling my life.*

58

Letting it Happen

> *In 1979, ten years after a spanking new magazine
> called The Mother Earth News had featured an article
> of mine detailing my intended breakout from the world
> of daily servitude, it seemed a good time to write a ten-
> year assessment of how it had all gone. Ownership was
> changing at that time, however, and the new team did not
> want my assessment. But this book seems a perfect place
> for it, as my central thesis (and quite possibly the basis
> for their rejection) had to do with the magic encountered
> once one is off the track of a controlled life. In fact, it was
> very much the same as the 'hitch-hiking way of life' that I
> speak for in this book.*

Ten years ago, I wrote a long article for *The Mother Earth News* (Issue #3) on 'How to Retire Six Months Every Year'. It was an outline of the principles that would enable me to live comfortably, working only half the year, on the ordinary earnings of a computer programmer.

I was all set to follow this program for the remainder of my working years — assuming that at age 42 I had quite a few ahead of me. But it has been eight years, now, since I've worked as a programmer or at any other normal kind of gainful employment. Eight years of no job, no regular income, no pension, no investments, no social security or welfare. And eight years in a variety of comfortable living situations, from mountain to seashore to big city and small town; sometimes in a group context, always with the privacy of my own sufficient quarters, and always in full command of my own time.

Right now, I'm in a mountain cabin near Calistoga, a hot-springs resort community about 80 miles north of San Francisco. Woods trails all around me, swimming hole and hot tub just a short walk away, and I've paid no rent here for the past year and a half. Before this, it was a year in Carmel-by-the-Sea on a no-rent basis; and before that, I spent two years in one of Berkeley's better residential districts, occupying an elegant indoor/outdoor studio for only $85 per month — a rental that I afforded by means of donated funds for a small sporadical.

John Shuttleworth has asked me to describe, in a couple pages, how all this has come about . . . what personal techniques and secrets I can pass on to Mother Earth readers.

Well, the secret is so very simple that it's not going to take any two pages to tell (although it may take all of that to persuade you that I'm not kidding). All it comes to is: Stop trying to make things happen for yourself, and *let them happen to you.* It sounds so easy as to be ridiculous, but in fact it is probably the hardest rule you'll ever try to live by.

I am not yet a master of it. Every now and then I still get it into my head to 'go out and do' this, that or the other. More often than I'd like to admit, I am caught short by a sudden sense of resistance to my movement; or a moment's flash that it isn't *this* door opening for me, but that other one over there.

Consider, for instance, how it was that I found myself moving to Carmel. My $85 Berkeley rent was becoming a bit burdensome, and was in fact being raised — a sure sign that some change was in order. With no bright prospect in view, I laid plans to go bicycling in the Sierra foothills in search of a new and likely abode. But first there was a social call that was tugging for my attention.

It happened that there was a lady doctor I had not seen in nearly 30 years, who had once treated me for tuberculosis. Quite by chance I'd learned that she was now in Carmel involved with an energy healing program that was of some interest to me, and a brief correspondence had brought an invitation to visit. There being no finer place for some pre-cycling relaxation, I was off on a junket to Carmel-by-the-Sea.

In the course of those few days, I accompanied the doctor on a treatment visit to a charming little old lady who'd had an incapacitating stroke not long earlier. She lived alone and was badly in need of some constant in-house attention, and . . . well, one thing led to another, and I soon found myself with an agreement to occupy a perfectly suitable garage-room in full exchange for my salutary presence. The exchange was drawn so that I was not bound to any rigid schedule nor obligated to any fixed amount of service — I was more like a guest-in-residence. And thus, you see, my world of 'letting it happen' let it fall nicely into place, before the bicycle plan could side-track me.

It has been this way more times than I could possibly recount; I believe it can be this way for everyone, but for that nagging impulse to plan and direct our lives. It surely stands to reason — if your boat is heading upstream toward some intended destination on a pre-planned itinerary, you seldom bother to linger with the surprise that waits around the next bend. You never let yourself experience the beauty of just letting it happen.

In the past few years, I've followed a journal practice of noting the unexpected events that come into my life each week. In the course of it, I've discovered that my life actually revolves more around these 'providences' than around any kind of plan or schedule I set for myself. Let me tell you, for example, how I came to see the great solar eclipse of not so long ago, which would not be visible within 500 miles of the cloud-bound California area where I live.

A month before the event, I was headed from Calistoga to a Bay Area hospital for some minor surgery. Not owning an automobile, I take what transportation happens to turn up, and this time it turned up with an old friend, Lowell, not seen in more than a year. Lowell brought a light plane into the small landing field at Calistoga — a surprise, because I only knew him as a land-locked truck driver without any hint of future wings. But ready as always, for the moment's happening, I flew the short hop back to the Bay Area with him — after which, we got to talking about his wish to build up flying hours and my wish to see the first total solar eclipse of my life.

Even as the day arrived it was uncertain, for the entire west coast was blanketed with a solid cloudbank, all the way to the Rockies. But Lowell made the decision to go – as far as Montana if necessary (and it was) – barely 24 hours before the critical moment. Off we flew, over Nevada, over the magnificent Tetons, over Yellowstone, to rendezvous with a two-minute solar event the next day — but no ready plan for overnight shelter.

Montana was layered with snow, and it was dark when we got there, and the motels were jammed with people who'd planned well ahead. But barely two months before all of this, I had met a couple who live in the little town of Roundup, almost dead-center in the path of the eclipse. So we ended up with warm lodging and hospitality that night, and very clear skies the next morning, and we saw what we came for. The magic of just 'letting it happen' had come through for me again.

But as I say, it's easier desired than done. Vowing to live in the here-and-now, and actually doing it, are as far removed

from each other as ... well, maybe as far removed as vowing
to conserve energy and actually giving up your automobile
— which is not really a far-fetched comparison, because it was
the giving-up of the automobile that probably led me farther
down this pathway than any other single change I've made in
my life. It brought me into the world of hitch-hiking; and so far
as I've been able to discover, hitch-hiking is about the *only way*,
in today's pre-planned world, that you can fully open yourself to
the Providence of the Universe.

If I were to set up an instructional course in *Letting it
Happen*, it would probably revolve around the hitch-hiking
experience. For it permits no possible control over events, no
possible prediction of developments — which is probably why it
is so frightening to so many people.

Well ... an exception: you can always say "no". And even
this turns out to be instructive, for the apprentice in living-in-
the-world-as-it-happens soon learns that this veto power is, in
fact, the only real power in life that any of us actually has. What
hitch-hiking further teaches is that we grossly over-use this one
choice of ours, in the ordinary course of things.

I recall one time when I was hitching with a friend toward
Utah. We were just outside Reno, on the threshold of the great
Nevada desert, and my friend, Scott,* had made me properly
wary of the risks of getting stranded in mid-state on this highway.
He cautioned that we should hold out for a ride clear through to
Salt Lake City, as cars don't often stop on this desert expanse
for stranded hitch-hikers — not even near the sparse few towns
along the way.

We turned down one ride of 40 miles, and then another
offer of 25, and finally a third that was going only 15. By now,

* Yes, it's the same Scott I wrote of in Section 2, but here's the story in a
better clarified philosophical context.

several hours had passed, and I knew I was looking at one of those situations where there is something to be learned from the resistance to movement. What came to me was that we should not be exercising this veto power, we were denying the Providence of the Universe. I talked it over with Scott, and we resolved to take the next ride, *wherever* it went.

It might have been predictable: an old desert sourdough in a cranky old pickup came along and lifted us for all of 10 miles, out to a 'nothing' crossroad. Scott and I could only laugh at each other, but we were game for it. In less than thirty minutes, the ride to Salt Lake City came along! As if the point of it needed emphasis, the driver told us that he had passed by another hitch-hiker at the very same place we'd been standing all morning; he hadn't stopped because there was a parked police vehicle nearby, and he didn't want to risk a citation.

It has been a long time, now, and a rare circumstance, since I last turned down a ride. What I've learned is that the Universe is to be trusted. Even though it sometimes seems to lead down crooked pathways there is good purpose to *everything* that happens. This may very well be the prime truth you'll have to learn and believe in, if you want the Universe to shower its fortune upon you.

And don't think this is just my own derelict fantasy. I have it on some very good authority, that it's so. Here is how crusty old John Quincy Adams, our sixth president of these United States, put it in his 66th year, in a September journal entry of 1833:

> *"I can scarcely recollect a single instance of*
> *success to anything that I ever undertook. Yet,*
> *with fervent gratitude to God, I confess that my*
> *life has been equally marked by great and signal*
> *successes which I neither aimed at nor anticipated.*
> *Fortune, by which I understand Providence, has*

showered blessings on me profusely. But they have been blessings unforeseen and unsought... I ought to have been taught by it three lessons: 1. of implicit reliance upon Providence; 2. of humility and humiliation, the thorough conviction of my own impotence to accomplish anything; 3. of resignation, and not to set my heart upon anything which can be taken from me or denied."

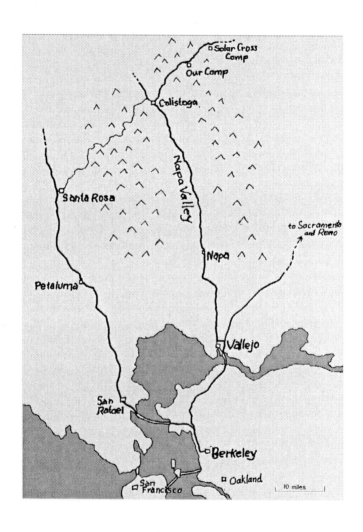

Intimations of Revolution

*As the hitch-hiking experience begins to open up
new reality vistas, it also breaks down one's easy rush to
judgement about what is real and what is surely fanciful.
In fact, it brings one daily closer to the world of the non-
rational, and to a healthier appreciation of its tempering
influence on the runaway rationalism that runs our world.*

*This account of how it was happening for me was
written for a Spring 1982 issue of Black Bart to update
readers on new developments in my world during the prior
year and more.*

Predictions and prophecies, prophecies and predictions.
Basically, I don't believe in them. My skepticism arises from
much too many 'disappointments' — which is perhaps a less
than best word choice here, because if some of those predictions
I've watched had come true this might be a hairier world than it
already is.

There was Clarisa Bernhardt's absolute assurance that
THE Big Earthquake would hit southern California on March
8, 1978 (...she who is said to have foretold, precisely, a number
of smaller quakes). There were those folks who had been
persuading people, a few years earlier, that they knew exactly
when and where the UFOs would land, in whole fleets — a
date now long past. There was even the grand flop of Comet

Kahoutek, which had been pre-ordained a real blazer by the supposedly reliable scientific community.

One of the ground rules learned from my own observations of reality is that we never see exactly what's coming. We might see all around it, construct reasonably accurate landscapes in our mind's vision, even correctly understand the scenario about to unfold — but a pre-view of actual times or events we are invariably denied.

How, then, should we regard the circumstance that credible prophets from all cultures and times (Nostradamus, Edgar Cayce, the Hopi Visions, etc.), joined by today's psychics and seers, are uniform in their prediction of a time of tremendous upheaval for these late years of the millennium? . . . that such predictions are bolstered by what is known of long-term cycles of social unrest, and geophysical change? . . . that major earth and climate changes seem, in fact, to be underway, if one follows the news and reports of such things?

And how am I to accommodate the series of strange and seemingly predictive events that have happened to me, personally, during the past eighteen months?

Those events of which I write began in the November days surrounding the 1980 presidential election — began with an unusual hitch-hiking journey from Berkeley to my home in the mountains, about 80 miles to the north. The trip had been delayed several days by a series of minor things, as though it were perhaps waiting for some 'right moment'. On the morning I finally stood roadside I carried a small sign saying 'Napa', the town that would cue drivers to my route. It gave me the advantage of all traffic on the main highway to Sacramento and Reno, and it ordinarily got me to the desired cut-off north of Vallejo, from where Napa was easily reached.

On this occasion, however, I was offered rides going west instead of north — a longer alternative way home, and one that doesn't go at all near Napa. After turning down two such offers, I realized that 'something else' must be happening, and decided to accept the very next ride, wherever it might go. And, of course, it went west, to the small community of Petaluma. It was the most roundabout way of getting me home, as the map shows — like tracing the curve of a crescent moon to go from point to point.

More accurately, I was let off at the freeway entrance close by the town of Petaluma, which is where a freeway hitch-hiker plies his mode of travel. This particular entryway was a tight half-cloverleaf, and another old fellow already occupied the shallow space that was there for gleaning on-ramp rides. Respecting the unwritten rule of the road, I spotted myself farther along the traffic stream, almost out on the freeway. But it was no good for either one of us on this afternoon, at this spot. I presently decided to edge just onto the freeway — risking the wrath of the highway patrol.

But there proved to be no time for that sort of calamity. I had no sooner made my move than a high-riding covered pickup flashed in from the fast lane, passing me by a hundred feet before it dusted to a stop. I ran to catch it. It was a young woman who said something about getting a 'message' in an instant glance from me — a message I hadn't known I'd sent. Adding wonder upon wonder, she was driving north to Santa Rosa, and then east to Calistoga and up the very mountain road I lived on! She would take me right to my door.

What developed from this strange and unlikely event was a friendship and an introduction to a group called Solar Cross, whose camp was where this woman was headed. It was a camp well-hidden on the mountainside, just a few miles from where

I live — not intended for discovery even by local residents. As I would soon learn, there were interesting reasons why they maintained such a low profile.

A week later, on invitation, I shared a dinner with the Solar Cross folks and found them to be quite ordinary and hospitable people except for one small oddity. They claimed to be in touch with UFOs and to have received from them a timetable for the flooding destruction of the state. It was to take place in the upcoming year of 1981, and they talked about it in the calm and matter-of-fact voice that one might note in a discussion of next year's weather prospects. I expressed my skepticism, and they took it quite in stride, allowing that there was room for doubt. In other words, they were believers but not fanatics. They were there not to escape or barricade themselves, but to be a high-ground haven for any who would flee the cities — after all, somebody had to be acting responsibly with the knowledge they were sure they had.

I did my best to suspend the natural doubts, because I had been led to this strange camp by a clearly extraordinary set of events — enough to imply meaning of some sort in what was taking place. And besides, these were clearly well-intentioned people, and intelligent by all indications (making allowances for their particular obsession). One fellow near my own age learned of my interest in the *I Ching* and he produced what looked like a pocket calculator for my examination. It was a battery-run electronic *I Ching* device! One button starts the circuit flowing, and another stops it, setting any or all of three lights to a red, green, or flashing condition, from which the *I Ching* hexagram is determined. One question, of course, was heavy on my mind, and I silently asked it and pressed the buttons: *What is my connection with this Solar Cross group?*

The response I received was *Break-through!* A rather portentous hexagram.

Back in my own quarters, the following morning, I asked the same question — thinking to eliminate any chance that the electronic gadgetry might have warped my connection with the Universe. I threw the coins and this time received *Revolution.* Remarkably close in substance to *Break-through*, and reasonably confirmatory. But what left me shaken was the moving line that came with it, line number three.

The third line of this hexagram counsels that a change is certainly about to take place, but it cautions against either undue haste or excessive hesitation in heeding the warning. And it footnotes (in my Wilhelm/Baynes text) a reference to Goethe "... in which the phrase 'the hour has come!' is repeated three times before the great transformation begins."

Whew! What in heaven's name could it mean? What three signals should I be alert for, and what sort of 'revolutionary' transformation is it talking about?

Twice during the next few months, on hitch-hiking returns to the mountain, I was similarly side-tracked to Petaluma in the same crazy way: while holding a sign lettered N-A-P-A. Realizing, now, that something extraordinary was going on, I was watchful on these two detours to catch whatever might further fit the puzzle. On one of these journeys I saw nothing at all to add to the picture. On the other, I picked up a shiny flat hand-wrench from the roadway, 7/16 size and indicating on its cast-alloy surface that it was drop-forged in India. It might only have gone into a toolbox, except that in the further course of the journey home one driver spoke of having been in the city for treatment of a "wrenched back," and another told a tale of how he had once hitch-hiked to . . . *Crescent City.* So the wrench seemed certainly to have some significance.

All that India meant to me was a friend named Priya who had been at the Rajneesh ashram in Poona for five long years and seemed likely to remain forever. The 7/16 could be read as a date — either July 16 or the lunar equivalent on a Chinese calendar, which would work out to August 14, give or take a day. Dates down the line to keep my eye on.

A few weeks later, browsing a bookstore, I ran into a slim paperback with the very unlikely title of *The Gentlemen of 16 July.* It was all about a French bank robbery, and I saw no earthly connection with anything of relevance in my world except perhaps my recent small inheritance. For awhile, I considered withdrawing my money from the bank before those two worrisome dates arrived; but none of this had the clarity or impact that it seemed a real signal should have. Perhaps it was only a confirming second synchronicity.

The date of July 16 came and passed, with nothing of any consequence to be noted. August 14 had much more prominence, being right at the peak of summer, a generally hazardous time in my season-oriented world; and also (spare a day) a tenth anniversary of that Friday-the-13th when all of these adventures were set in motion by my departure from the world of straight. But still, there appeared to be no connection with what Solar Cross was all about, nor any of the expectable impact conveyed in those nine-months-earlier *I Ching* readouts.

The weeks and months moved on, my mind far into other trips and activities, and this whole strange business fading back into those nether corners of the mind reserved for unresolved experience. I was preparing a late Fall issue of *Black Bart* and getting ready to participate in a right-livelihood conference, and on beyond that was a grand mid-November celebration of *Black Bart's* tenth anniversary. In fact, as these events drew near, it became apparent that they'd be clustered on three successive weekends, and I was starting to refer to them as the Big Three that would wind up my year of activity.

Suddenly from out of blue-nowhere, I received word that Priya had left India and was on her way to California. She would arrive in time for the anniversary celebration. It took awhile to hit me that this event was number three of the Big Three. It took a longer while for me to know that the day she actually reached here, November 6th, was precisely one year from the date of my original hitch-hiking diversion to Petaluma! Quite suddenly, the whole Solar Cross business was alive again, up front in my consciousness. But I was not at all prepared for what came next.

It was Friday the 13th of November, the day before my celebrational weekend was set to begin (and an eerie reflection of that Friday the 13th earlier noted, of August 1971; in fact, I had first met Priya on the very job that I walked away from on that remembered long-ago date!). We were experiencing the worst storm in the four years I have lived here — winds and rain whipping against the old mountain lodge without let-up.

At about 3 p.m. – maybe on the very dot of it, my attention was not on the clock – a cluster of three huge oaks close by the lodge were blown down across telephone and power lines, landing on our twin propane tanks and releasing a geyser of uncontainable gas. Our three primary and essential utilities crunched by three trees at 3 p.m. — a triple whammy! And I recalled the omen of the oracle: 'the hour has come'...repeated three times before the great transformation begins.

I realized in a flash now, too, that it was *the third time in the year* that falling trees had touched my life too closely for comfort. Several months earlier a massive oak had cracked at its middle for no apparent reason, and come within inches of crunching my cabin; and on a beautiful early spring morning with no wind at all, a towering evergreen in town had dropped – similarly without apparent reason – uprooted, within a mere hundred feet of where I was walking.

Trees! TREES!! *The very word resonates with the oracle. And this time, there is no question of impact.*

It is clearly conclusive: a circular set of signals, each acting as a pointer, each confirming the last, each emphasizing the impact for even a halfway alert observer. But still, I might only guess at what it all means.

Is it possible, dare I surmise, that this is my way of seeing, confirming what the seers and psychics say? Is it possible, November being the seedtime for the coming year, that the Great Transformation is underway — only now becoming visible in this springtime's gradual thaw? Has this exceedingly heavy winter, not yet past as I write these words in mid-April, been the difficult but promising labors of a great new era just being born?

I don't know. I report to you only what I've experienced. I do not believe in specific predictions . . . and yet . . .

It certainly marked a transformation underway in my own world, and entirely unanticipated at the time this was written. In locating a Berkeley residence for Priya, as 1982 unfolded, I also found one for myself in Berkeley. And then, in the next few years, Priya played a key part in my eventual relocation to Seattle, which opened a whole new vein of rich ore in my evolving life — as will be seen.

Upping the Risk Ante (1984-85)

Here is another pair of shorties, their commonality being the documentary record of a transitional moment in my life when I was pushing toward greater risk in my hitch-hiking.

By the mid-1980s, I was fully aware of some deeper flow in my life, and a barrier I had to somehow get across before I could fully tap into it. That barrier was represented by a stasis that I seemed to have settled for: my alternative life had become so comfortable and secure that I was stagnating in it. Events, themselves, conspired to get me out of it and over the barrier, but not without the help of some prodding realizations.

I recognized, for one thing, that I was fast approaching an age when the normal trajectory of events would rob me of my continual dalliance with insolvency: I would attain my entitlement to Social Security.

I know it will seem strange to many that I should look upon this with any degree of apprehension. But I was aware by now that insolvency puts risk into life, and risk translates as the medium in which Providence functions. Or put another way, the extent of risk that can be accepted as a concomitant to one's life is a fair measure of how readily one will observe Providence at work in it. The trick lies in learning to accept risk and not try to avert it by asserting control — which is precisely the conditioning one receives from hitch-hiking.

It had long been a dream of mine to put myself out on the road in an open-ended journey, with virtually no funds, just to see what would happen . . . to see how the Universe would respond to me in such circumstances. And I realized that any possibility of my doing that would be foreclosed with the attainment of my Social Security entitlement.

Here, then, are two short tales that chronicle my move in this direction. In the first of them, I try a journey to northern Oregon in the summer of 1984, taking no money (to speak of) with me. The second piece is a letter from the following spring, just as I sent it, detailing for friends some of what transpired for me – once again in Oregon – when I finally set out on that open-ended journey that so intrigued me.

The 'contacts' I make reference to in that letter were folks on the Black Bart mailing list, many of whom I had never personally met.

Episode 6.1

...with Empty Pockets

It had been about two years since I'd last tried my luck on the road, and I was a bit unsure of what to expect from it, so I allotted four days to the 600-mile-journey. I also gave myself a handicap I'd never tried before. Since I have the prospect ahead of me of being on the road with unusually shallow funds, I thought I'd make a dry run, so to speak, and I left town with only $1.17 in my pocket, but plenty of foodstamps so that my actual daring was minimal.

I'll spare you the humbling detail of the first two days, which saw me only as far as Sacramento – barely 80 miles out of Berkeley. They were the worst two consecutive days of hitching I have ever experienced, and I was going through all sorts of head-trips trying to account for it. Had I lost my touch? Had the highways tightened up that much in two years? Was it perhaps a journey I should *not* be making, after all? Everything has meaning — the only problem is to figure out what the meaning is.

I finally decided it was a rigorous rebuke of my efforts to control the journey by turning down rides that seemed poorly directed, and by holding a destination sign, which is another way of being selective. I figured this out after the first discouraging day had netted me the single late-afternoon ride to Sacramento; but I was now at a Sacramento interchange freeway ramp that went off in several directions – mainly back to the Bay Area – and it seemed just ordinary prudence to have a sign saying "North". The prudence, however, had gained me not a single ride during the entire second day, and I had now to consider that I was still being too choosy. It was either that, or to abort the whole project.

So on this third morning I abandoned *all* effort at control and stood ready to take whatever should come. If it took me back to Berkeley, then it would be my message from the Universe. *Any* ride at this point was better than none.

In hardly 20 minutes, a car pulled over for me! The driver peered out and asked where I was headed — and I told him I honestly didn't know. He thought about that for a bare moment, and then said he was sort of lost, himself. There was not much use in standing there trading uncertainties, so I just got in at that point and we took off. Could I have known it, my entire autumn journey to The Dalles on the Columbia River rested on that one moment of absolute faith. Well, it turned out he was going north — 90 miles toward Oregon.

I knew immediately that I had figured it right, and had broken through the psychic barrier. Nothing would hold me back any longer, which was exactly the case. In five rides that day, I would travel close to 500 miles. But the sweetest measure of the day's breakthrough was yet to come, on another freeway ramp further up the line.

This was outside of Red Bluff, about noontime. Encountering three other hitchers there, I took my proper place, the last one down the descending ramp. The fellow closest eyed me in hungry misery as I began to enjoy the entrée of my just-purchased lunch — a cup of yogurt. He had the doleful look of a dog that just watches you while you eat, and I finally had to give him the bottom half of the yogurt. His expression barely changed as he welcomed it and finished it.

Almost immediately, a small car pulled past all of us and stopped just on beyond me. Now, the rule of the road is that the lately-come hitcher is last down the line, but if a car stops precisely for him there is no contest — it's his ride. I was halfway into the car when I again caught that utterly devastated look of the sad character that had just finished my yogurt. The driver, in my moment's hesitation, spoke up — quite unnecessarily — to say that he could take only one rider. I made an instant and unprecedented decision. In a flush of both confidence and conscience, I got out and motioned the other character into the car. After all, he had been waiting much longer than I, and I *was* now in the aura of a perfectly functioning connection with The Universe.

Well, in hardly any time at all a 20-mile ride came for the rest of us — and I was on my way to the second half of this amazing demonstration of one of the oldest and most basic of Biblical certitudes, variously rendered as 'casting bread upon the waters' or 'give and ye shall receive' or simply The Golden Rule.

My very next ride was with a van-loaded family of Seventh-Day Adventists. Prompted by nothing more than their own charitable instincts, they left me with a large, freshly packed bag lunch when we parted company 60 miles up the line. And now, the most incredible touch of all: along came *the very driver whose hospitality I had earlier given over to that hungry soul with the sad-dog eyes, two hours and 80 miles back along the freeway!*

This driver had paused for a swim in Lake Shasta, lost his sad-soul passenger to the road at that point, and decided to finish his journey alone — but stopped for me, now, only because he remembered the incident and recognized me. It was his ride that took me all the way through Oregon, assuring completion of my journey within its allotted span of time.

There's a lot to ponder, in that chain of events. Never before have I travelled fully without funds; never before have I, myself, been so generous on the road; never before has The Universe gifted me with such precisely clear validations of faith and charity. I think miracles only happen to those who put themselves entirely on the line — I think this is the great and lovely teaching that life has for us.

Episode 6.2

...easing into Homelessness

Cottage Grove, Oregon
April 22, 1985

Hello to all:
    ...from Central Oregon. I'm waiting out a storm that
has put me into some real winter weather (even snow)
for the past five days. It puts the limit on my slow trip to
Seattle.

    Luckily, my hosts in Cottage Grove have an Atari word-
processor ... and in the cabin-fever of this long 'downtime'
I drift back to the technology I've foresworn. A hopefully
excusable inconsistency.

    The journey thus far has been a real conditioning
process — one test and challenge after another, with a kind
of graduating intensity that has kept me on the edge of my
ability to accommodate these changes. In fact, this storm
— and my utter sense of isolation with its arrival — nearly
blew out my circuits. But I found the narrow passage to a
haven, with that serendipitous precision that seems to be

81

my particular blessing. One thing that came to me, not so long ago, is that people who seem to be innately lucky are somehow able to tap into their right-brain intuitive center when the chips are down.

My first night out of Berkeley was spent at Sherman's, in Fairfax, and the following morning his friend, Carter Rose, picked up a poorly formed but recognizable quartz crystal in front of Sherm's house and gave it to me. It was like an omen for the journey's start. I went on from there to visit people in the Santa Rosa area, and spent my first night truly 'out' in a central Santa Rosa city park. From there, it was over the hills to Helen & Shaw's place on Cobb Mountain, and then to Harbin. These were the easy breaking-in days, before I began to get my road legs.

I think it was my 9th day out when I found myself hitching on Hwy. 101 at River Road, north of Santa Rosa. Two hours there, the previous evening, and now another in the early day, and I was beginning to feel the impatience of waiting-time, and wondering also what it meant — for these instances often carry messages. Perhaps they *always* do, if only we could know. Staying in one low-traffic spot for endless hours is not a flow but a stagnancy, and I flipped a coin to see if it was time to start the walking journey. The coin said "no." I sensed an inner disappointment, and then I remembered Donna's psychic reading, before this journey began — that I was supposed to get beyond "exterior oracle aids" on this journey. So I shouldered my pack and headed for a parallel and walkable roadway. Hardly a hundred feet from the spot of that decision, I picked up the most beautiful and perfectly formed crystal, the size of a very broad thumb, that I have ever been rewarded with!

It set a tone for the rest of my trail. Nothing could possibly go irremediably wrong. In the next two days, I walked 25 of the 30 miles to Cloverdale, reaching there in a 90-degree mid-afternoon heat with blistered feet — but everything was okay. I got a ride, then, to Boonville, right into the driveway of friends there with whom I spent several recuperative days.

Back again on the road, I set my pace in earnest northward — after first reconstituting my bothersome blister with a 5-mile 'stroll.' But it was still okay; just part of the conditioning process. Made it to Arcata that evening — actually to the needle-in-haystack Westhaven residence of my ex-Berkeley friends, Lois & Matt, which I could never have found on foot, but to which I was taken by a thoughtful driver who found more fun than trouble in the search.

Late start, next day, and an acid-spaced driver, who reminded me of nothing so much as Jack Nicholson, took me on an unbelievable (unrecountable) ride clear to Coquille, OR (and clear to midnight). Clouds and sprinkles were gathering by next morning, but I made it to the main (I-5) freeway outside of Roseburg before the sprinkles slowly became showers and the showers slowly became rain.

In Oregon, you can stand right on the freeway and hitch, so I figured I was surely 'home free' — possibly all the way into Portland. But the only thing I got, there, was wetter and wetter. Finally, not being able to understand this at all, I trudged the three soaking miles into Roseburg, phoned my one unlikely contact in that town, and discovered he was in no shape to put me up. Now I was really confused. Four hours to dark, a definite frost in the air, soaked clear through — and what to do?

The options I was willing to consider: a Lighthouse Mission in town, or a busride to either Cottage Grove or Eugene, 50 and 75 miles distant, where I had contacts. I shied from phoning either of these for reasons that would make little sense to any rational person. I settled 'blindly' on Cottage Grove, and in retrospect I think it was the only choice that could have afforded me a week-long welcome and a much needed rejuvenative space. I picked it even though I had never met Steve or Karen. My bus got there after dark, twenty minutes behind schedule, yet just in time for my phone call to catch Karen as she arrived home.

In some ways, being housebound here is the biggest test of this journey so far. It is forcing me to confront a driving urge to keep moving, which, if not diluted, could ultimately drive my energy into the ground. I've got to learn to take rest and shelter — here, there, anywhere — with as much composure and ease as I accept the open road. It is the basic contest between Being and Doing, focused in my life now as never before.

What I glimpse in this is something of a very fundamental human dilemma of our times. We are all driven — either to achieve or to excel or to acquire or to create. We do not know how to just BE, to accept the present for what it is. This is what makes meditation so difficult for many, what makes time-off something that can only be handled in small doses. And I daresay it's a major element in the world's present confusions around unrestrained growth and the terminal limits of space and resources. I don't know where the line is to be drawn between a healthy level of creative achievement and an obsessive, destructive level — but I do suspect that we are cultural victims, all of us, of a loss of clear perspective on this. Being forced to live a day-to-day life — as I now am — may be the best of all contexts for coming to terms with those impulses.

There is a certain 'strangeness,' in knowing I have no fixed-base home, that is very hard to describe. It flits in and out of consciousness like a butterfly, telling me nothing at all very definite. It is perhaps the very vagueness of it, a kind of delicate insubstantiality, that defies capture. It is sort of unreal, and makes my sense of life accordingly now unreal. The many anchors of living an ordinary, regulated life are probably ways of the left-brain to maintain its hold on our being, and I imagine that I slide quite easily now into a right-brain, almost dreamlike existence.

It affects my sense of time, very definitely. There is nothing expectable in each day's pace now — I am often amazed at how time seems to linger, or events to 'stretch out,' whichever best describes it. Again, there is never any sense of time passing either too slow or too swiftly — it always feels right. Events of recent times seem to fade back endlessly into the past.

However and regardless, with journey itineraries to try and meet, I am still too anchored in a time-context for my own satisfaction. One day this will drop away; and I cannot even surmise what that experience will be like.

Until next time...

The Summer of Infinite Presence

Here is the longest tale in the book, written as a
special report for my Black Bart readership. It covered
a particularly special journey — the one in 1985 that
was my plunge into homelessness on a full scale (I had
no home to come home to), and my ultimate relocation
to Seattle from the Bay Area. I had no intention of
migrating at the time; I was just 'on the road' for an
indefinite and open-ended period, letting it happen as it
would, until my anticipated return to California — which
proved, in the end, to be only a way-stop.

I think you'll find this to be something more than
simply the recounting of a hitch-hike journey. I hope that
it will stir you to think about a few things, as I hoped it
would for those to whom it was first offered. Oh, and by
the way, you should find a couple sections of it familiar in
the reading, for they develop the same tales as were told
in the second Episode of Section 6. You might even enjoy
comparing the two, to see how I reworked some of it,
including the realization from it that had not yet occurred
to me when that earlier letter was written.

Well, I have seen the elephant — as was once said of certain
great journeys of discovery. I have been four months at
full departure from my old Berkeley haunts — hitching my
way around the country, an increasingly road-wise 'roadie,'
riding and residing with all kinds of people, tasting the flavor of
America, 1985.

My hosts have spread the spectrum: students, farm and construction workers, salesmen and truck drivers, teachers and writers... I've stayed in homes with backyard swimming pools and homes with backyard toilets, ridden with people who needed gas money and others who bought me meals, some who would put the fear of God into me, some whose country-twang talk almost called for an interpreter... but one thing had they in common: the willingness to help a stranger on the road or a weary friend at their door.

I have seen, too, the more typical side of our times: the steady flow of mainstream isolation that passes a hitch-hiker by. Out of fear, out of an inflated sense of privacy, I could never be sure — but they gaze at me with a bland and indifferent curiosity, as if seeing a strange creature of uncertain classification... as perhaps I am. There are not many such as I on the road today, pleading passage, claiming the alms of roadside charity. It is an unseemly vocation in affluence-driven America, 1985.

Vocation? ...or vacation! It has been both for me, and much more. Exploration, education, stimulation, fascination... I tread the ever-anxious tail of conventionality; I exchange yesterday's me for someone as yet not too clearly defined. But then, such definitions are not to be framed in mere weeks, months. They cannot be declared, only slowly sought and uncertainly created. All I can account for at this midway point of passage is the grist that has gone into the mill. Draw no conclusions just now, for my own are likewise only tentative.

I wanted no definite plan or itinerary for the journey. Yet, such enclosure has a way of erecting itself from a few preliminary commitments. Innocent promises to be in Michigan by June, Minnesota by July, and back in California by August provided my summer's limits and largely determined which friends I would spend time with. It was a counter-clockwise tour: down the California coast, across the southwest, up through the farm belt east of the Mississippi into the land of sky-blue wa-a-ters, and back across the Rockies by a pre-arranged ride through the country's midsection. Most of my time was spent between east Texas and Minnesota, the largest single block of it in St. Paul. I had preceded this main run, however, with a brief 'warm-up' trip (an April joke!) into northern California and southern Oregon.

I've stayed with 32 households, six of them for a week or longer; have spent only about one night in six on the 'open road' (not sheltered in a host home) and, in fact, did almost all of my actual hitch-hiking in the first part of the journey. I've only spent two days 'on the road' since mid-June.

But facts are barren. They don't even begin to touch the sense of this journey. Where I went, who I met and stayed with, is almost immaterial in itself. The real thing I want to put across in this accounting is something I probably cannot even capture in words, let alone by facts and statistics. If I can ask your indulgence I'm going to make something of a collage of this report, paying little attention to proper sequence, maybe even varying the idiom of my approach... a series of episodes focusing on some invisible point, and let's just see what happens.

* * * * *

Some sequence, of course, has to be respected, for the journey had a beginning that set the tone for much of what followed.

"Trust your instincts," my friend, Donna, told me. It would seem that I should not need that advice, for I have often enough given it, myself. But I was asking her, in a psychic counseling session a month before the journey, what it was all about? Where was I going... and most of all, why?

89

She told me that I could not know any of that, except as each step is taken. That this journey would be, in fact, an introduction to the very art of listening to my own inner voice and coming to trust that it will be there precisely when needed. That I must learn to give it precedence over all other plans, and even over my oracles (the *I Ching*). The one, after all, is The Real Thing; the other, merely a vehicle for getting to it.

I took it as I take all such counsel: tentatively, and pending some further clarification as to what it all meant. For the moment, it confirmed me in my several years of search for ways to tap into right-brain awareness. I have wanted to get closer to this source or 'receiver' of the spiritual impulse in our lives. I have been hungry for any bit of information, any exercise, which would help clear the roadblock of Words that keep obstructing Truth.

It came to pass, then, that on the morning after my very first night out of Berkeley, I happened upon an imperfectly formed crystal about half the size of a forefinger joint, discovered in the yard of a friend. I took this as a positive omen for the journey, for there have been crystals along my way, found or given to me, ever since this decade and this present trail began.

I have found that synchronicities often come in pairs as a way of emphasis, much as if to say: okay, once can be coincidence, but twice is something else! Eight days after the discovery of this first crystal came my moment of confirmation. I had been lingering among friends in the north Bay Area and was ready to take longer strides toward Oregon. But I found myself suddenly stalled at a freeway entry north of Santa Rosa. For three hours, broken by a night's roadside rest, I had been waiting there. It was not a terribly long wait, but the passing traffic was discouragingly bleak.

I played with the idea of walking up a parallel roadway. It seemed, from a hitch-hiker's perspective, a bit foolish — but not, perhaps, for one who was 'living on the road.' It would erase my boredom and lighten my spirits, and what care had I for time? Yet, there is always an impatience to contend with on the road. I finally had to flip a coin because I couldn't decide.

The coin told me to stay right where I was. I felt an instant pang of disappointment, informing me of what I really wanted to do! But, gee — hadn't the coin always given good advice? Or had it merely released me from the burden of going any deeper than my ambivalence. I suddenly remembered Donna's counsel. I smiled at my precious indecision, shouldered my pack and headed at once for the walkable highway.

Not a hundred feet on my way, I looked down to see a quite unbelievable second crystal. Big as a fat thumb, perfectly formed and 'crystal clear,' it was an absolute jewel of personal validation. All that day and the next I walked — 25 miles, through blistering feet and 90-degree heat, hardly concerned with the discomforts. I gazed repeatedly at this marvelous crystal, as I lay in soft grasses beneath shade-towering trees... as I paused by trickling creeks to cool my feet. I was never more sure of being on my path.

* * * * *

If experience is sometimes a stern teacher that we are justifiably wary of, then synchronicity is surely its playful, lively counterpart — but a teacher, all the same. It has followed me all the course of my journey, whispering wordless messages, alerting me many times to things I would otherwise have given scant notice, helping me to frame my own truth. Sometimes it seems only to be 'having fun' with me. But I know it doesn't fool with us, it is always saying something.

When I came back through Wisconsin for a second time, on my way to connect with a cross-country return-home ride, I spent the night in the Madison office of Basic Choices, an alternative network center run by John Ohliger. He always has interesting books lying around, and I picked up one this evening — I'm not even sure, now, of the name of it. Perhaps it was *The Psychology of Transcendence*. It was a thick volume, devoted to the methodical evaluation of paranormal and otherwise out-of-the-ordinary experiences that are generally associated with mystical and altered states of consciousness.

I turned to a section on synchronicity and read about how the rarity of what we call pure chance may not after all be so rare. Coincidence, says the author, may be more ordinary than we think. He describes two experiments that can easily make the point: the common-birthday game, and the small-world phenomenon.

On the birthday game, he notes that in any gathering of more than 23 people it is statistically likely that at least two will have the same month and day of birth. The odds for such a 'coincidence,' he says, become a 50% possibility when the guest list reaches 23 — a number far fewer than most of us would suppose.

The small-world phenomenon is an exercise that demonstrates how a package may be delivered to someone entirely unknown to the sender, anywhere in the country, in only 5 or 6 person-to-person transfers, if each such transfer is directed toward a person who "might reasonably know" either the addressee or someone who *could* know him or her.

Concluding these impressive illustrations, the author closes the passage with a quote from one Randall Collins: "Trust the experience, not the interpretation."

Wanting to know something more about Collins and his quote, I followed the footnote reference to find out that it was taken from a book edited in 1977 by John Raphael-Staude. I recognized the name immediately. In 1977 I was living in Carmel, and John Raphael-Staude visited me there! — the only time in my life I have ever had contact with the man.

"Trust only the experience, not the interpretation" — and especially not the interpretation that so easily dismisses such interpretations.

* * * * *

As if someone other than you – *anyone* other than you – can mediate meaning about anything at all! The history books, the newspapers, the government — do they provide meaning, or is it something that happens inside yourself? How much less likely, then, is the truth of your own world to be found in anyone but you?

And maybe, then, you should consider *the extent* to which you can establish meaning in your world. But where does one find guidelines for establishing meaning, if not in the meaning provided by others? Well… maybe in the careful cultivation of synchronicity, itself.

In the winter months prior to my Berkeley departure, I became vaguely and almost incredulously aware that the rainfall would cease whenever I really had to go out of my house. It was so unreal that I hesitated saying anything about it — but it seemed to be true, and I wondered if it might be the promise or evolvement of a special kind of Providence that is obviously of great value to someone on the road.

At first, as I wandered through northern California in the still-wet month of April, it seemed to be so; the charm held true. But then in Oregon it failed me. I was thoroughly soaked in a steady downpour a few miles outside of Roseburg. My presumptions were dashed, and I became extra-cautious about rainfall thereafter; but I wondered at the curious reversal and continued to reflect on it.

The following month, as I headed south and east on the longer leg of my year's journey, I was almost constantly under threat of rainstorms and thunder showers — and the old charm seemed to be working again! Many times the rain would appear to alternate at the same tempo as my intermittent lifts — I'd be riding through rainfall, but thumbing on a dry inter-stretch; or I'd have a country tavern on hand at the precise moment I needed cover. Even on those evenings when a rainy night was the sure prospect, some magical roadside shelter would appear. One time it was the covered arcade of a produce market, closed for the weekend; another time, the provident appearance of a yacht harbor with an unlocked cabin cruiser up on chocks, to crawl into for a perfectly dry night's sleep.

As I thought more about the events of that earlier Oregon occasion, I finally brought something else that had been happening that day into the context of my reflections. I had been in repeated proximity to another man who was also hitching into Roseburg, but only because he had been held up and robbed at a coastside Greyhound depot. He was burdened with heavy luggage, had no money at all, and had never hitched before. I gave him ride-priority and a certain amount of encouragement, but I might have provided some real support — like sharing food stamps or the food I was carrying, or even helping with his luggage (for it was dragging his ability to find the best road spots). We who expect charity from the Universe (and who does not?) must learn to recognize those occasions when it is expected by the Universe *of us*! I came finally to 'understand,' you see, that because I hadn't, in this instance, done all that I might, I was rained upon.

Who's to say whether we discover such uncommon cause/effect relationships or create them — or that there is really any difference? It is interactive creativity with the Universe. We 'change our world' in such ways, and become then bound by what we perceive — or conceive. We open a mythic path for ourselves.

So I followed this insight. I considered myself as much an agent of charity, thereafter, as its recipient, and shared as I was able, through six amazingly dry weeks (for me) of frequently stormy weather. Day and night, the charm sheltered me. Until I reached the far border of Michigan, where something went wrong again. At Escanaba, near the Wisconsin line, I walked out of town to where there was no possible shelter, and got dumped on by a sudden cloudburst.

Where was my error? I hadn't been uncharitable in any manner that I could see. But I did see something! I saw something in synchronicity that had no connection at all with being charitable — and at this point I made a leap of 'understanding' that would not be warranted on any connective basis; it can only be accepted within the realm of a mythic path. Earlier that day, I had overstepped a sexual boundary. I don't wish to share the details, but I must mention the point because it is deeply woven in the themes of the journey.

I'd had a roadside 'adventure' that morning. I was involved with someone in a way that seemed situationally okay to me at the time; but now, in the bath (the cleansing?) of my first drenching in more than 3000 miles of open-road travel – in the illuminating light of this mythic compact I had made with Spirit and Nature – the only possible conclusion was that I had erred.

What I am saying, you see, is that the world, on an open road (on any open road, be it literal or metaphoric), is capable of being a pathway of messages – of either confirmation or denial – for those who let it be so. I have read, in anthropology texts, that the primitive tribesman lived in constant fear of nature because he had no control over it. Much to the contrary, nature was a bible to the primitive tribesman and he had need of no other. Its 'ten commandments' were written in storm and earthquake, rainbow and eclipse — while we moderns have split this intimate and sacred dialogue into religion and science, and discovered only that we 'control' nature to the approaching climax of our own destruction by it.

Yes, you can argue that it was all superstition; that we have 'proved' how storm and rainbow are mechanically accountable and have no bearing on Truth or Spirit. But I will argue, in turn, that I have proved (to my own satisfaction) that they are message bearers!

You can say that I have only 'invented' messages of convenience to my own morality and values — but I will say, in return, that interpretation has never been anything but a subjective experience … that the world has never had any other meaning than those we've invented and decided to live by. So how can one meaning (the moral one) be put down, in favor of another (the scientific)? *Play the game that your heart feels best with.*

* * * * *

This was exactly why I wanted to go on the road in the first place. To break away from the framework of life that says reality is only as our left-brain insists it is.

Right-brain – where the rules change completely – is no match in persuading us of its Truth, in a world that left-brain has

96

built and daily reinforces. But if we once find a way to break the mold... !

And the mold, of course, only exists in our own heads, and only for so long as we continue to play its games (which seem to make such 'common sense' that we remain trapped in their endless circle). But now I know... now I know...how easily the circle and the mold can be broken...

Here is another slice of my journey, written for another publication:

Me and Bruce rode out of Tyler, Texas on Friday the 24th of May. Not together — we didn't even know one another. I was hitch-hiking; he was pulling an extra-long house trailer on what must have been a two-ton pickup, if they make such things. I was four hours ahead of him, because we had to get to Linden, Texas – 90 miles up the road toward Nashville – at the very same time.

Don't ask me how it happened. It just happened. My first 30-mile ride advised me to stay the hell out of Louisiana — weirdos and bad roads. My next ride was going right on into Louisiana, to Shreveport, except that he was short on gas money. I gave him a couple bucks, just enough to get him there, but I didn't go the distance with him. I remembered the other fellow's warning. Still, I wouldn't have gotten as far as Marshall if I hadn't fed the gas tank.

The third ride was easy — it came right out of the Marshall gas station where I drank a coke and thought about the long walk to the other end of town. You never hitch going into a town, only coming out of it. But this dude knew what I was about and took me 40 miles on, to Linden — where I found Bruce gassing up for his next 90 miles of trailer haul.

Actually, Bruce found me. Said he'd had long enough, there, to look this old hitch-hiker over, and realized I might make an interesting passenger. If he'd seen me roadside, he told me, he'd never have stopped for me. Now the really wild part of this is that we'd both arrived back there in Tyler on the very same day, a week earlier, and we'd both left there this same afternoon. And we'd both reached this service station at the same time!

Bruce and me rode halfway through the night and halfway into next day — all the way to Nashville, 500 miles. Like me, he lived on the road, except he was doing it legit. He repaired microwave-tower antennae, hauled his home from job to job, one week in Texas, the next in Kentucky, the next... while I was just bumming around, trying to understand what things are all about these days.

We talked, Bruce and me, all the way into the night — about every damn thing you could think of. Jobs, women, football, guns, hitch-hikers (yeah, Bruce had a real loading on hitch-hikers and how dangerous it is to pick them up), money, getting ahead in the world, religion, reality... That's where we finally settled — on the question of reality and what makes things the way they are.

That's when I found out how he and I had been matching pace, into and out of Tyler. But it wasn't so surprising; I've been having things like that happen ever since I left California. I've been watching it — sort of like a hawk watches everything going on in the grass down below, until he knows he can strike for a piece of nourishment. And he gets it!

Yeah, watching reality happen is kind of like looking for my nourishment. There's a lot more going on down there than anyone would believe — both for the hawk and for me. And it isn't so simple or straightforward as the boys with the measuring tools would have you think.

I tell Bruce, outside of Memphis, that reality becomes just about whatever he believes it will be — and that's a hard one for him to handle. He can't quite hack that big a hunk of nourishment. So I feed it to him in smaller pieces.

"Hey, now — you know a guy finds pretty much what he expects to find in the world, right? Things work for him when he's willing to take chances, or they don't if he's too uptight. The ones who are afraid of life are the ones who get beat up by it."

"Yeah, that's for sure."

"And you get just about what you give, right?"

"Can't argue that!"

"Well, so where the hell does what you expect – the same as what you put out – come from, but out of what you believe?"

Bruce didn't talk for a long while after that one. Maybe ten minutes of road-rumbling silence, while he chewed on it. And he couldn't spit it back at me.

"You know," he finally said, "that just might change a lot of my life around."

* * * * *

Which brings us, I guess, to the most essential tale I have to tell, and possibly the most elusive, and the one I know I'll have most difficulty in finding the right words for. Partly because I'm not fully clear, yet, on what it's all about. But there are other, and more involved reasons for this hesitant opening: I am treading an area that is like a minefield, booby-trapped with internal sensitivities and prejudices that I fear most of us don't even suspect are there.

I wonder if any of you have ever thought about the most hidden face of prejudice and bigotry in this country — where do you think it is? We're pretty open about our racial and ethnic prejudices, these days, and pretty easy with ideological and political ones — I mean, we argue them, but we acknowledge them. But what about religious prejudice? Not so bad, you say? No problem?

Well, I'm going to stick my neck out and say that every one of us is a religious bigot!

I say it, because I've discovered that I, myself, have been one for years — beneath my liberal/progressive/radical veneer. And I say it because I don't know of anyone who can openly consider it (of themselves). Yet I hear it every day, in the flashes of innuendo about born-again Christians, about Catholics, about Rajneeshees, about — yes, even from Unitarians, about atheists!

And how do I define religious bigotry? The same as I define any bigotry: it is not a question of acceptance or tolerance, or even 'loving thine enemy,' it is thinking that one's own way is somehow more enlightened. Because it is this relatively minor bit of pride that results in putting other people down, unless we catch ourselves on it.

This tale is not about the discovery of bigotry — that is only a by-product. Yet, it may be the ultimate meaning of the tale, I'm not sure it isn't. It's a tale of my own deliberate effort to suspend bigotry, to drop my barriers of resistance long enough to see what would come in as a result.

It was only in the few months before my journey began that I copped to the fact that I did, indeed, have barriers of resistance. I have been beset for years (I will avoid saying plagued) by encounters with fundamentalists and born-again Christians – mainly outside of my personal friendships, but they were finally beginning to appear within that circle – and I consistently regarded them as accidental and meaningless encounters. I finally realized two things: one, that I was making a large and unwarranted exception to my general belief that all things in one's world have personal meaning; two, that I was putting a fair amount of energy into warding the input off.

I saw, too, from last year's experience around Rajneeshpuram, the nature of undiscovered bigotry in almost everyone I know, and did not want that sort of self-poisoning, closed mind to be a part of my makeup. It hides, usually, beneath the guise of 'critical analysis' — but it is bigotry, pure and simple, when it leaves no possible room for a positive evaluation.

So I resolved to open myself, on this journey, to whatever of a religious nature (as opposed to what we New Age separatists call spiritual), might come in on me. Any and all denominations, any and all levels of expression.

The course of exposure was marvelous: a Passover Seder in Santa Rosa, a born-again (and formerly Jewish) hitch-hiker near Cloverdale, a Lutheran service in Boonville, a bible scholar in Cottage Grove, a mystical-Catholic service in Monterey, a Unity lay-preacher (ex) in Sedona, a Pentecostal service in Kokomo, a Unitarian minister in Traverse City ... all over and everywhere, I talked with people of every persuasion, read parts of such books as seemed appropriate, was given Bibles (yes, plural)... I even checked into a tiny wayside chapel in northern Michigan, and bought my foods at Seventh Day Adventist stores along the way.

But again, the facts say nothing. Let me tell you the trend of my experience.

The Lutheran service in Boonville came shortly after I had embarked from Berkeley and it cued me in a rather interesting way. It just happened to be my birthday, and the pastor addressed his sermon to the wisdom of Doubting Thomas! I had pushed myself to be uncritically open, and here he was telling me that skepticism is not such a bad thing after all.

The 'motion was seconded' a few weeks later in Monterey. 'Father Charlie' is a very special and off-beat Catholic priest. He does an unorthodox Sunday service in his own home, and the small congregation assembles around a magnificent quartz crystal centered in his living room. He, too, spoke of Doubting Thomas, and 'crystalized' my willingness to maintain skepticism.

But I was finding myself, at the same time, more open to talking with people about Jesus and Christianity than I had ever been before. In the Sedona conversations with Dick Fishback, I came to see that there is no essential difference in the reverence expressed by many toward Jesus, by some toward Rajneesh, and by myself toward what I simply call Spirit. Nor is the apparent effect of this reverence much different in the lives of any of these 'devotees,' as near as I could tell. There is the same uplift and the same blind submission – the two sides of the devotional coin – in all; even in myself.

It gave me a sharp jolt of self-critical reflection. How could I maintain my own beliefs if I suspect the fallacy in those others? And yet, it makes no sense to move back into atheism, for I have seen and know too much about the reality of Spirit. But ... I can't go on patronizing myself about "that fellow's obsessive devotion" as I turn right around to continue prating my own.

I could see, too, that for all its 'failures' in history, the Christian Church nevertheless has provided the sole institutional support (to my knowledge) for an ethic of Love and Charity and Forgiveness. This is not to be lightly dismissed. That its practitioners fall far shy of the vision is a separate matter and does not, in itself, reflect unfavorably on the ideal or its vehicle, nor certainly on its source.

Outside of Albuquerque I was accosted by what seems to have been the very last of a long line of 'bible-belting' Fundamentalists intent on bringing me the Word of the Lord. (The very fact that he was the last, of a fairly steady stream over the years, has me considering, in the light of what subsequently came to pass, that I may have finally 'gotten the message').

I was completely receptive to what he had to say to me, even to the Bible he pressed on me, but afterwards felt more than a little confused about what I should be seeing in all of this. I feel no need to be 'saved,' feel no inner impulse at any level to become a part of this mass movement toward a Christian heaven — so, what in God's name (so to speak) is it all about? In the futility of that moment, I made a slight, perhaps desperate, 'offering.' I said that I would consider it my message if, at any time in the course of my journey, a properly ordained minister of any faith or denomination should pick me up. Because in 14 years of more and less hitch-hiking, I had never, to my knowledge, received a ride from any such. (Which is interesting in itself.)

A day later, I was rescued from a barren stretch of New Mexico interstate by a young college student who wanted mainly to tell me of his newfound respect for Mormons — because of their wholly charitable act of repairing his automobile, which literally permitted his continued journey across the country. He had suffered an ignition-system failure, and the cost of a garage repair would have forced a choice between leaving the car behind or not getting home. He was ready, himself, to convert to the Latter Day Saints.

In Tyler, Texas, Elihu Edelson provided an interesting model for me of a man who is able to embrace all faiths and linger on none — maintaining his prime focus on a mystically spiritual New Age. Elihu turned me loose for a week in a library with much provocative material, including something called The Urantia Book, which I can only reference, not describe.

In Kokomo, Indiana, I went into the Fundamentalist aspect as deeply as I could go. There lives Alison, a longtime correspondent who was 'born again' in the years after our friendship began. We have been a thorn in each other's side many times — but the correspondence has somehow been maintained through sometimes long lapses. Now, I bathed myself in two days of nitty-gritty dialogue with her and husband Terry... along with visits to sundry born-again friends and a Pentecostal Sunday service.

She first challenged me with the question of whether or not I believed in God. I gave her all of my neat evasions — some of them Unitarian, some of them atheist/agnostic, some of them my very own. In the end, it finally and simply reduced to my discomfort with the word, God, and its suggestion of a heavenly being. I could acknowledge, however, that I don't believe in a mechanical universe, nor in an accidental one... therefore, words and labels and intellectualizing aside, I must certainly believe in something that, with liberal fairness, translates as God — much to my own surprise!

I was particularly curious about the Pentecostal service. I wanted to see what these people were like in their worship. Well, they are like any other denomination, essentially. Reverential, supportive, loving — even reasonable! That is to say, there was very little in the sermon that I could find to challenge. And I was beginning to see something, now, that hit me with a good deal of impact.

All congregations (Jewish, Pentecostal, Unitarian, etc.) express, within their ranks, the same fundamental ideals of love, faith, sharing, charity, and mutual support. But outside of their ranks, they engage in a subtle warfare with almost every other faith, over the precise and correct interpretation of the 'WORD' — and we are right back, again, with the problem of Words being roadblocks to Truth. The Truth, in this case, is what people express as *feeling* (toward one another, toward their God and their ideals), and as faith. The Word, in contrast, is the rational and intellectual analysis of how it is structured and

104

what it all means. And we wield these Words that distinguish one denomination from another with all the grimness of an apocalyptic battle — completely losing sight of our common grace within Spirit. I think it could be said, fairly, that Jesus brought a basis for spiritual unity to the world, and the Bible has eroded it with words.

With this realization I could see, finally, why the right-brain need not and cannot speak to us in words — indeed, why it dare not! Spirit and Words are simply of two different realms, as mutually exclusive as church and state. I could also understand why the Old Testament insists that the name of God cannot be written or spoken; and, as well, the injunction in the Tao that "the way that can be described is not The Way."

I found myself confronting a Unitarian minister, a week later in Michigan, with this very challenge: to cease 'chasing the mystery.' He could agree with me (or I with him) that the mystery cannot be touched by intellect. He, however, upheld the effort to do so, while I, now seeing the mischief in it, would back away.

Outside of Green Bay, Wisconsin, a few days later, came the encounter that I didn't actually believe I was waiting for. A busy stretch of freeway with big trucks pounding by, and a seedy-looking old Cadillac angled through them and stopped for me, way down the line. An unimpressive heavyset man, perhaps my own age, not very communicative, but we exchanged pleasantries and trivia for about 15 minutes until I finally asked him about the big, well-used Bible sitting on his dashboard.

"Oh, I'm an evangelist preacher," he said, without making any fuss over it.

"....Do you mean..." and it was a long pause, as I carefully picked my words, "Do you mean you're an ordained minister?"

"Yep."

I had to practically drag it out of him. He was Jim Hyde, a non-denominational evangelist out of Green Bay, heading right now for a Pentecostal Church across the state to do his thing. He was also founder and president of the Revival Fires Evangelist Association.

I needed to know, then, why he picked me up — and I probed him as thoroughly as I could, trying not to be impertinent.

"Just an impulse," he insisted. He seldom picked hitch-hikers up, but he saw me and felt he had to pick me up.

"Was it, like...a 'divine' impulse?"

"Well," he lingered on it, "...I really can't tell the difference."

He took himself so easily, so naturally, that I knew absolutely he was there for me. I told him, now, my own tale (not a word of it before this moment). He seemed only moderately impressed, and we immediately got down to three hours of the most rock-bottom religious and anti-religious discussion that I was capable of finding words for. I laid all of my doubts and skepticism before him, in absolutely plain English.

In retrospect, I can't believe how little of that 3-hour conversation remains with me — except for the impressions. I do know that I felt thoroughly vindicated in my own spiritual path by this evangelist, and at the same time fully accepted by him from where he was coming from. Let me quote from my own road-journal, written the following morning:

> "He was so beautifully validating of where I'm at, and
> what I see, that I feel he was really heaven-sent! The
> entire non-denominational bit, in the first place, his
> criticism of Pentecostals, their unnecessary 'speaking in
> tongues,' the limitations that each sect imposes on its
> believers, the accent [foolishly placed by many] upon

106

wealth as a sign of devoutness, etc. He agreed with me
that the focus of any real spirituality is God, not Jesus.
And said that Jesus, himself, had always maintained
this. I told him quite frankly that I just cannot speak,
or relate to, a Christian vernacular, and he said it
made no difference at all – that the temple is inside
each of us and that our own inner light is the ultimately
true guideline – that no man can teach [another]
outside of that.

"...I spoke of my inability to 'ask Jesus into my heart'
– as is always urged by the proselyters – that I felt
no need for it, and insufficient spiritual freedom in it,
and he somehow gave me to understand that in this
very quest of mine I had, in fact, 'let Jesus in.' The
realization both shocked and pleased me."

My apology for the lack of literary refinement, but that is
'raw data.' My expressed surprise was not so much at anything
he said (except for that last note), but that I should hear these
things from an evangelist — and, of course, that it was so clearly
a gift on my own quest, asked for and received.

But remember what I said about synchronicities often
coming in pairs. Barely a week later, still in Wisconsin, I
was picked up by a second minister! This one was a retired
Methodist preacher, eight years older than I, and he was just as
precisely 'for me' as Jim Hyde, but in an outrageously different
way. This old-timer, as grizzled as I, had just the week before
hitch-hiked from Tennessee to Wisconsin, even by much the
same route as I. I found more of my own nature in him, and it
was as though the Universe had thought to balance things out a
bit, in giving me the doubled blast of a confirmed synchronicity.

So what does it all add up to, this unlikely sideshow of
my journey? Am I being born again? Am I turning into a
Jew for Jesus? Am I copping-out on my years of level-headed

detachment from all things smacking of fanatic belief? Am I making some new and possibly questionable commitment?

Probably no to all of the above — but I'm not sure that all the data is in yet, or that all the right questions have been asked. It is very clear that something has been happening in my belief-structure, even if I am unable as yet to define it. But let me roam a bit through some speculations that aren't so black-or-white as the above, and see if I can give you a bit of what I do newly feel on these matters.

We of this century who have steered clear of religiosity have done so because it had become sterile and hollow — made the more so, perhaps, by a world in which science became enshrined, and money too: the twin 'religions' of our secular age. In the excesses of these two idolatries a spiritual impulse was bound to re-emerge, as all things seek a condition of balance, sooner or later. It emerged in a variety of forms: Fundamentalism in the Near East, a surge of eastern mysticism in the West, the 're-birth' of Christianity among those, here, not inclined toward mysticism — very few of us have not felt the impulse in one form or another.

Yet we have failed to recognize its basic underlying commonality; we have begun, once again, the age-old squabbles over who's got the right vision — the same tensions that have led, all through history, to religious wars, inquisitions, pogroms.

I think my perspective, now, is to move away from this question of who's got the right vision. I think it's time, now, to allow *every* vision — what's more, to encourage every vision, to respect and even participate in all of them. Isn't this, after all, what we're trying to practice in our civil affairs? In our domestic affairs? Should it be any different in our religious affairs?

And as with all the rest of those, I think it has to start 'right here' in each one of us. Yes, I accept Jesus Christ! — even though I'm still a Pantheist. Why not? He and I stand for most of the same things in life. And if Jim Hyde's world can embrace me, mine can embrace Alison — whether she feels that way about me or not. Let's go for it.

* * * * *

Just as Nature and Spirit provided me with a pair of crystals to certify the start of my journey, I was gifted at its end with one of the rarest phenomena, I'm quite sure, in all of nature. A moonbow!

Pat Nelson and I were coming in toward California from the eastern side of the country, both of us to attend the first national Holyearth/Earthsteward's gathering. It was the night of the 2nd full moon of July – what Pat calls the night of the "blue moon" (because it comes only once in a ...) – and we were on one of the lesser highways coming out of Nebraska and into Colorado, looking for a campsite.

Actually, the entire evening was a display of natural spectacle: first, an incredible sunset, behind and around towering storm clouds with horizon cloud lines so thick and dark that we were sure they were mountains, until they began to distort and fragment like pulled taffy; then the storm itself, and its silent sky-rending lightning flashes; and then, as darkness intensified ahead of us, the full moon rising in a nearly clear sky to our left-rear.

We angled south now, and suddenly, in the pitch-black of the storm-center out my right-side window, I saw a pale white arc — grey would be closer to the truth, grey and ghostly with about 60 degrees of arc. It made no sense to me. It was not the light of anything I could imagine. We parked to look at it, and it finally struck us what it must be! Sure enough, the arc could be vaguely traced all the way across the horizon and it was exactly opposite the full moon, now an hour's height in the sky. We stood clear of the van, and our own shadow, rendered by moonlight, neatly bisected the arc above the horizon — as is true of any rainbow.

This was a *moonbow!* A sunbow (which is a true rainbow) is supposed to have been a special covenant sign between God and the Jews, according to the Old Testament; and it strikes my fancy that a moonbow may be one for the present age, where we've had quite enough of the sun's yang influence in the world and perhaps need a moon-covenant to bring things back into balance.

* * * * *

It was, in all, a lovely summer too swiftly gone, and yet endlessly present. A kind of time-passage I have never known before. Events of the very recent past seemed to be forever ago, and the near future had no reality at all.

It was a summer of infinite presence.

Derelict Days in the Northwest

*The book's title piece is very little concerned with
hitch-hiking the road, proper, but it may very well provide
the best illumination of what the hitch-hiking Way of Life
can look like.*

*This tale picks up where the previous one left off.
It was written as a retrospect, five years later, to bring
friends up to date on what had been happening in my life
since departing California for the northwest. It is a tale
about 'riding the rapids' of life — casting one's self right
out into the flow of things, and letting the gods take over
from there.*

*I don't think you'll be disappointed — though you
may find yourself thinking it's a piece of fiction before
you're through, rather than factual reportage. But I assure
you, it is merely the way life can work for you, if you can
only stop holding the handlebars so tightly.*

A gypsy life may have its problems, but the boredom of being
tied down is not one of them. This tale properly starts back
in the midyear fluidity of 1985, on my return to California from
a country-wide and summer-long road trip in order to attend
the first annual Gathering of Earthstewards, an affiliation that
grew from my longtime friendship with Danaan Parry. I had no
idea of the marvelous consequences that would unfold from that
occasion.

I had committed to remaining on the road, you see, until fortune should favor me with a satisfactory winter residence — and a winter's lodging had in fact already been offered in Santa Barbara, on California's warm southern coast. So, being free of anything more demanding for the moment, I took advantage of the move Danaan and the Earthstewards were making to the Northwest, that I might enjoy what remained of summer's lingering warmth on Puget Sound — and (not incidentally) perhaps reconnect with a woman I had met the year before at that place of ill-repute in north-central Oregon called Rajneeshpuram, where I spent a few fascinating weeks of the previous summer. I offered to help with an issue of the *Earthstewards Journal* in exchange for temporary shelter, and it all fell nicely into place. At the last moment, I even scored a free ride north practically to Danaan's doorstep.

The weeks passed enjoyably on Bainbridge Island without remarkable happening, right up to the eve of my intended late-October return to California. I was all set to leave, piggy-backing on a ride going south, when I got last-minute word that the hospitality in Santa Barbara would fall far short of a winter's extent. I had to make an almost instant choice between stranding myself down south or remaining stranded right where I was.

For some reason, it seemed to make more sense to hang in with an existing unknown than head for a new one. Never mind that northern winters are more severe, and that my network of friends was far more substantial in California. I could number the people I knew in the Seattle area, at that time, on one hand's worth of fingers. But the weather was still seductively nice in Seattle. And so was Madelynn's proximity. Besides which, the last-minute nature of this development – giving me no time to think anything through – could be taken as a pretty clear signal to hang-in. I could surely stay a little longer, and something else might turn up.

What did turn up was a crazy bunch of oddments: driving an Earthstewards vehicle, one day that Danaan & Diana were both out of town, I got tagged for lack of a current *California* vehicle registration! True, it was their problem, not mine; but it developed into an unbelievably complicated situation, adding up to a $112 fine that someone would have to pay, unless I stayed around to contest it in court — though my welcome as a house guest was wearing perilously thin.

To compound it further, the great November snowfall of '85 left a sudden blanket of foot-deep white that was to last for two weeks, putting a complete closure on any lingering thought that I might still hitch-hike back to California. The full fact of the matter was that I couldn't even afford a return trip, by now, in any other fashion. Of course, I hadn't anywhere in particular to go, even had I the money for it. Somehow or other, I was going to have to find my winter's lodging and sustenance in the northwest.

I picked up the scent of a trail from a poster on the wall in a local foodstamp office — a poster first seen, actually, on the very day I'd gotten the citation. It was a call for "mature women" to work as live-in caretakers for the disabled and elderly. That's reverse sexism, thought I to myself . . . why not a mature man?

The trail took me through several inter-related social service agencies, each one recommending me to the next, and the last one suggesting that I go consult the Co-op bulletin boards. It had begun to feel like I was being shuttled along in a brush-off conspiracy, but...there it was, at the end of the line, a posted notice from a rather remarkable young woman incapacitated by multiple-sclerosis who needed a weekend assistant caretaker. This, I thought, would be perfect; it would give me the wherewithal for the rental of a modest room somewhere in town, and who could complain about two days of responsibility a week?

But the easy scenario was not to be; it was only the sweet nectar of the flytrap. By the time our connection was made, Jean needed a fulltime attendant — not just two, nor even five days a week, but six, at 24 hours each! I tried to back off, but her persuasive powers found a ready partner in the insistent urging of my own desperate situation. She offered live-in room and board, the free use of a van, and a salary of $600/month — a virtual goldmine to one who had spurned wage-labor for 14 years! In one sudden catapult I'd be home free for the winter.

No, not exactly free. Can you just imagine the carefree easy-rider that was me, being suddenly flipped into total responsibility? My innocent freedom of such long attainment was going, in one simple step, from all to nothing-at-all. That California New Age talk about the earth suddenly doing a pole-flip had come true!

The reason Jean was remarkable was that she proved to be a kind of 'psychic vortex,' around whom all manner of connections seemed to happen, though she was entirely unaware of this magical capacity and mostly given to wrestling with the miseries of her own fate — but then, aren't we all? Although I stayed with her only the five excruciating months of that winter, I met people coming through her household who were to weave in and out of my future affairs for years to come. Jean, herself, would be a resource for me at critical later stages of this transition, not leastwise for the ever-ready use of her van as a 'moving facility,' as I house-hopped from one northwest residence to another over the succeeding few years.

That winter was surely my Northwest (Rite of) Passage . . . my come-uppance from a principled resistance to the world of work into the pragmatic, survivor-focused opportunism that was necessary for what would follow.

When it came to its end, a funny set of early-year happenings typical of my season-ordered life induced me to rent a nearby room and pursue that perennial fantasy of writing a book on my enlightening adventures. February's ever-reliable 'sprout' came this time as an invitation from a friend in Santa Cruz who had achieved board-member status on a small foundation that made minimalist grants to obscure but worthy projects — an invitation from her to submit a proposal if I had any good use for a couple thousand dollars.

I thought of the ever-present book project, of course, and formulated a proposal on it. The proposal didn't get anywhere, as it later turned out; but having turned my focus toward such a possibility, I soon realized that I *already had* the funds for it, in the money socked away while I was taking care of Jean.

Life just seems to work that way for me, nowadays. Everything is part of a Grand Weave, and the sprouting events of February (of every year) invariably seem to translate into a pattern of activity, whether by some inherent design, as I truly believe, or simply because I take them as such and pursue their possibilities. I do think that things happening at this time of year have a peculiarly heightened potency. But it is only one instance of the many sorts of 'signals' that alert me to something going on in the weave of my life.

Consider, for instance, what happened on the way to my next residence. There was a small but fascinating ad in a local paper for living quarters available to "writer, artist, or scholar living on poverty level." It had only a postbox address, so I sent a response and waited...and waited. Meanwhile, I discovered first-class quarters – but (for me) expensive – just a block away from Jean's. I took an option on it but continued to wait for the other to materialize in the form of some response. I waited several weeks, and finally thought I'd better go claim the more expensive one. It was an upstairs room with a fine view of the snow-crested Olympics, in the household of a new young family — an ideal spot for a writing project to take shape. It even offered the use of a computer in an adjoining upstairs room!

Merely *minutes* after I returned from putting a sizable down-payment on the new quarters – and after those weeks of futile patience – a call came from the old fellow who had placed the earlier ad. It was such a clearly indisputable signal: the tight conjunction of events – yet there being no question as to the temporal priority of my sudden impulse to claim the closer residence – that I knew I had to go meet the fellow and see what it was all about.

Jim was a crusty old iconoclast in his 80s, an inner-city recluse who had simply pondered my response for a long time before deciding to call me. He had a full upstairs flat vacant, and was more interested to see it go to the 'right' person than in whatever income it should bring him. But it needed a lot of refurbishing if ever to be conducive to a writing mood, and I wasn't sorry for the way things worked out. Jim and I became friends, however, despite my having contracted elsewhere for shelter, and this friendship would be fruitful for me in due course.

I proceeded, after a short visit to California, to invest myself in the writing project. I still had no clear intention of remaining in Seattle, but I had no better place to be, or to do this thing, and I could count on a minimum of distraction in this environment where I still knew so few people. I tried, also, to find part-time employment to alleviate the rental drain on my savings, but nothing came of it. From any practical perspective it would seem to have been a rather indulgent waste of a hard-gained nest egg, but I was 'living by the signals' and sure something worthwhile would come of it.

Sometime in early July, about the time that summer's intensity begins to build in earnest, I sent a long, completed chapter off to a publisher who had already expressed some interest in it. My writing energy went with it, and so I took myself on a week-long bike and ferry jaunt to a jazz festival in the San Juans — mainly to while away the waiting time. On the return bike ride, I came down through Whidbey Island for the first time, and came to the shoreline town of Langley, the most perfect out-of-the-way living locale I had ever seen. I was instantly struck by a wish to live there...sometime, somehow.

Waiting for me on my return was a gentle but depressing rejection from the publisher. My summer had busted, and the one thing clear to me, now, was that the book had to go on 'hold.' I had perhaps two careful months of funds still left, at the rate it was going out, and would then once more be on the rocks of insolvency unless something were done in a hurry to prevent it. It was then that a rather strange possession took hold of me. I had seen Whidbey, felt its clear, strong pull, and realized that there were many relatively inexpensive cabins available there, and . . . by God, I would get myself back into the world of computer programming, that I had left so long ago, and it should not take me long to Make It Happen! It was a moment of wild irrationality, in several respects, but it powered a short, intensive, and totally absurd job search, which kind of served as a bridge to what came next.

Right in the deep-summer moment of early August, the time when either crisis or development characteristically peaks in my world, I received a letter from a longtime friend — a former resident of Rajneeshpuram, uprooted by the year-earlier dislocation there, who was in Arkansas slowly putting together a new stake for herself. She wanted to come west again and proposed that I find some suitable locale and quarters for us to set up winter housekeeping, as a joint project. I knew by this time, of course, exactly where to go. And it fell into place with such clean precision, for me, that there wasn't the least doubt of it being a properly ordained course of action.

Just a few miles from Langley is a New Age community called the Chinook Learning Center. I joined a weekend work-party at their Clinton headquarters, and put out the word in a potluck discussion group that I was looking for a place to rent on Whidbey. I learned, while there, of the almost immediate availability of an isolated five-room house, spectacularly situated on a bluff overlooking the ferry wharf — a dream of a place, at an affordable price of rental.

Affordable, that is, for Priya, my partner in this venture*
— for I was almost bottoming out by the time we actually moved into the place in October. And by the time our winter prep of household equipment and foodstuff was in place, even Priya's funds were looking under-nourished. But I had perfect faith that I'd secure some kind of employment, the way things had come together for us.

It didn't exactly happen that way. Priya did fine, setting up a catering service out of our kitchen. But I lurched along, through November and December, from one promising opening to another, with nothing ever materializing. It was almost uncanny, the way each bite on the line kept me hanging on the vision of landing a decent employment, as it diminished my energy for the further search. Bits of temporary work kept me feebly within sight of financial solvency but never quite close enough to it, and by January the tension was rising between Priya and me.

* This is, of course, the same Priya referenced in Section 5.

I had turned to the town of Everett, across the water from Clinton, in hopes of better prospects; and in the course of my job-seeking there, I tracked onto an agency called *Operation Improvement* that administered a federal program funding job-training for the disadvantaged — mainly high-school dropouts. Being, myself, a somewhat older and somewhat different sort of dropout, I nevertheless got into it and took their battery of tests, hoping I'd qualify for a word-processing class. It was in November, the year's archetypal 'seed' time, and I scored an unprecedented 100% on their nine-part, 3-hour exam, surprising *them* hardly more than myself. It was another strong path signal.

But in practical terms, it merely put me on a waiting-list, and time dragged on into January with nothing happening there (another good sign, had I realized it, since winter's nurturance of a seedling is always hidden from sight). In terms of day-to-day events it was simply discouraging. And while I could make some seasonal sense of it for my own encouragement, there was no consolation in that for Priya, who could only see that I wasn't holding up my end of the bargain. The mood between us went from sour to bitter, and it gradually became clear to me that I just wasn't going to hack it on Whidbey, despite all the good preliminary indications.

I extended my job search all the way into Seattle, an impossible stretch for a car-less commute, but a threshold for the disconnect that was clearly shaping up, from Whidbey and Priya. I did run across some irregular telephone-survey work in the city, which kept me in pocket money, but it wasn't enough to finance any such move, much less bring me back in balance on our deteriorating situation.

In the midst of these shifting energy patterns, in late January, the call from *Operation Improvement* finally came through: It was time, at last, for assignment to classes. On the face of it, this would simply compound my problems by cutting into my job availability time, but my hope was to qualify myself more reliably for employment. Word-processing seemed the most congenial possibility and the quickest to achieve.

It was a bit of a setback, then, to find out no word-processing courses were available this season — which was rather strange, because they had access to all of the region's community colleges and private vocational schools. But Victoria, my interviewer, looked over everything available and could offer me nothing more inspiring than a class in ordinary data-entry work, way out on the east side of Seattle, which I would not take.

Then Victoria took a long look at that incredible test score, and decided that she somehow had to salvage me. She said that if I could find *any course of study*, anywhere in the greater Seattle area, that could be completed in under a year and for less than $1000 in tuition and supplies, and I felt it would work for me, they would call it a special personal program and fund me to it!

It was a wide-open *carte blanche.* I immediately scouted out the community college scene – basically in search of word-processing – and then I stumbled across something of much more value to me, something I hadn't even suspected was out there.

A rather elegant community college, nestled nicely among tall fir greenery just north of the Seattle city limits, offered a three-semester program called VCT – Visual Communications Technology – essentially, the printing and publishing trades, including the recent development called Desktop Publishing. I signed-in for the spring quarter, to begin in about six weeks. And from a state-funded companion program administered by the Everett Senior Center, I was awarded a small personal stipend that provided almost enough for me to get by on . . . if I could just hang-in for the six-week gap before any of these benefits would begin.

Living on nothing was something I practically had a degree in, by this time. But I had to leave Whidbey to Priya. I moved back to Seattle, now, relying on the friendship I'd established with old Jim, who put me up in his still vacant upstairs quarters for nothing more than the cost of utilities. Daily spending money came in from the intermittent telephone survey work. I had to borrow bus fare now and then, and I still owed Priya $150 — but I was in amazingly high spirits right through that narrow passage, for the signal-beam was as clear and steady as one could ask. And there was no detour this time: right with springtime, in March, the schooling began.

Jim's place was only a stopgap shelter. It was poorly located for my daily commute and hardly comfortable enough to think of as home, although it was a blessing immeasurable for that brief destitute period of transitional need — there for me as if by some grand plan that had long ago been laid out. Indeed, what lay ahead for me in the progression of summer could hardly have been imagined.

My earlier benefactor, Jean, had by this time found a strong-willed caretaker named Michael King, one of the most amazing persons I have encountered on my northwest sojourn, and shortly after I started to school he found a new place for them to live on the northern edge of town — practically within walking range of the college I'd be attending. They not only had an extra room there, but Michael would welcome an occasional day or evening of care-taking relief, so we worked out an arrangement between us that was equitable all the way around. I'd have a free room in exchange for a modest amount of service to Jean, for which Michael even provided me a small slice of his own salary that would bring me, at last, to a sustaining level of income.

My classes all revolved around publishing technology, a strictly vocational program, in the surround of youngsters aiming for the broader world of career — a world I had long ago abandoned. It was a rather absurd situation. I was like some graybeard ghost of another time in their midst, as they were like ghosts of another time in mine. Thankfully, a few other oldsters were on campus to keep me in some reasonable degree of reality-orientation.

I used the opportunity to refresh my old computer familiarity, and probably jarred some instructors' preconceptions by my 'precocious' grasp of it. But most useful of all, in my perspective, was the course in Pagemaker, the desktop publishing process, for it gave me a tool I could really work with. Even before completing it, I had a commissioned job to put it to work on, assisting a friend with a 72-page booklet, which eventually (after a year of part-time labors) earned me $1200. But more significantly, it cleared me for an early departure from the obligation to complete the vocational program. It met the proof-of-employment requirement, just in time with my discovery of further academic fields to conquer.

Being in a college milieu now, it gradually dawned on me that the name of the game is educational grants and such — the financial-aid largesse practically unknown when I was a youngster (except for the GI Bill, which I missed out on).

Well, why not? I was set for spring, summer, and fall quarters; and why not go for an added financial boost in that last quarter, for which there was still time to submit a Financial Aid Form? So I sent one in — noting, in all innocence, that I was only requesting funds for the fall quarter, the last quarter I was authorized to attend. And *no loans*, I specified; only grant money or work-study funds would be acceptable. I wasn't about to be hamstrung by debt, at this point.

But the federal government does nothing by halfway measures. It was a bright June day (clearly recalled) when I got home from school and opened the letter of award — and was so stunned by it that I took it very lightly. I kind of laughed, and said to Michael, "Hey, they want to give me nearly $7000!" The award was for *the entire 1987-88 school year*, and it consisted of several kinds of grants including free tuition and work-study. No loans.

As I say, I was stunned. For two full days I went around thinking, "It's really too bad I can't make use of this." I was fixated on my obligation to complete the program I had begun. Finally, I began figuring out how I *could* make use of it.

By falltime, I had fully reshaped my program. The vocational one was brought to closure — properly satisfied by the afore-noted fulfillment of its conditions. For work-study, my newly-gained computer expertise was sufficient to put me back to work with Earthstewards, editing their now bi-monthly Newsletter at an exceedingly handsome rate of pay (subsidized, of course, from federal funds). And I now had a much more appealing range of curriculum choice – early literature, short story writing, art, etc. – and had begun to loosen up and really enjoy the experience.

By the start of `88, I was knocking at the door of the University of Washington. It had become apparent that there just wasn't enough for me, in either breadth or depth, at Shoreline Community College. As long as I had the funds, I wanted the richness of the university — if those funds were transferable. I went to find out . . . and the Universe handed me one of the most incredible affirmation signals of this entire northwest passage.

I waited in line, in the university's Financial Aid office, for one of three interviewers who were processing counter inquiries.

My rotational turn took me to a young woman who looked at me rather oddly and inquired if I had ever been in Everett. I looked closely at her, and *it was Victoria!* — the very same Victoria who had encouraged me, a full year before, at *Operation Improvement*, to go out and find a program that would serve my needs.

Such things are only the stuff of film-scripts, too implausible for reality. How can one possibly doubt, or feel the least shade of anxiety about, a path graced with such affirmation? So I put the transfer into the works — never thinking for one moment that it might not materialize. Yet, in doing so, I set in motion the one piece of bad business that could topple my whole crazy structure.

In registering at Shoreline when the year began, I saw no reason to labor over a full, detailed record of prior schooling, which had included some long-ago tries at getting back on the track of my abandoned education: two brief periods at a San Francisco community college, the most recent of them 27 years back. It seemed of no account for a strictly vocational pursuit. But now that it appeared I was actually going to resume that old path toward a degree, I needed to resurrect all those old credits to gain myself the proper university footing. Among other things, they provided me with the barely met requirement of a foreign language — Spanish. (Actually, my Spanish fell a bit short, but close enough to gain me a waiver for the fractional insufficiency.)

But there was a ghost lurking in those old records that I'd all but forgotten — a college loan that had never been paid back. I got word of it two months before the spring quarter was to begin — notification that my entire financial-aid process had been stopped dead in its tracks until I do something to clean the slate. It meant, of course, that my whole financial picture was suddenly frozen. I had to marvel that this had not happened to my earlier application for financial-aid, for the purely lazy reason that I simply hadn't bothered to mention that earlier schooling.

I didn't even remember the amount of the loan. It took several weeks and a phone call to Washington D.C. to find that out. An original loan of $800, it had increased by interest to $1420. I told them it was impossible for me to pay that off at once, that I needed some time for it (as if I hadn't already had 27 years!). But the woman I was speaking with made me a deal: she said they'd forgive the interest if I could come up with the $800 principal; and without hesitation, I agreed. I had that much left, of funds that the government had already given me!

The ordeal, however, was not yet over. There was still the matter of getting a clearance back to the University in time for the upcoming quarter. I waited...and waited. I was on the phone to D.C. a half dozen times, to no avail. My angel, Victoria, warned that I could find myself stuck with a tuition bill that Financial Aid would not cover (like another $800), if the clearance didn't arrive in another couple weeks . . . and when Victoria speaks, I listen! She was advising me to back-off and remain at Shoreline, where my financial-aid was still good, for another quarter.

As it turned out, she was right on target. But I was so intent on getting into the U that quarter that I applied her advice in a different way. I registered *at both schools*. I had free tuition at Shoreline, and their $950 Pell Grant paid my way into the UW. I took 22 credits, altogether, weaving the time in such a way that I could manage the logistics of it . . . whew. It was a sheer gluttony for punishment, but I was flying high now.

The summer of `88 was the only break I took for myself: an AMTRAK visit to friends in California and Arizona. After that, it was a straight two-year haul, right up to my Bachelor's degree in the *Comparative History of Ideas*. With that, the academic trip came to completion. One B.A. is quite enough for me; I haven't got time for anything more. Remember: I wasn't looking for it in the first place; this all evolved from the innocent search for a word-processing course, in the outflow of being flat-broke on Whidbey Island.

In that sense, it's been another sort of graduation, of possibly much deeper significance than whatever is represented by a B.A. It's as if I've completed a kind of 'finishing school,' here in the northwest — a culmination of many years at the study of learning how to let life lead me, instead of exulting in any ability to take charge of it, which is today's common mode. Just the other day, as I was bringing the details of this tale to their finish, a friend asked me what advantage there is, in letting the fortune of indicative events call the turn of one's path, as opposed to shaping it for one's self. I had already acknowledged to her my conviction that either method can shape a viable reality.

My answer was that the path laid out by Providence is, by its very definition, an easier one. But that, alone, is not sufficient reason for taking it, for there is hardly anything wrong with choosing a path of greater challenge and demand.

There is a more profound reason, however. We are damned, in this age of all possibilities, with a failure of faith. Nobody really believes, anymore, that there is such a thing as Providence, in any form that can be trusted to do as much for you as you'd do for yourself; or even to look out for you! We are intent on 'looking out for ourselves.' The ordinary caution of looking both ways when crossing a street has been lifted out of its proper context and applied to the vast array of life's unknowns, with the force of a compelling 'common-sense' imperative: be careful and purposeful, lest you allow something undesirable in life to 'run you down.'

So we live in a constant morass of insecurity — for to be always apprehensive is to be ever insecure. We insure ourselves to the hilt (or feel at constant risk if we can't); we agenda our lives to the day and hour, to keep the unexpected at bay; we commit ourselves to a future before it can even be seen. We live entirely unnatural lives in the firm belief that prudence dictates wisely. Yes, Prudence is the big 'P' of our lives, not Providence. And to this extent, we are poorer by far than our material wealth would ever lead us to think, for we live not in the idyllic grace of Nature's world, but in an isolating fear that passes for 'common sense.'

Here I am – a total material 'failure' – stumbling along life's path without any idea of where it will next take me; yet, in as profound a state of ongoing security, and freedom from anxiety, as ever in my life. I am, moreover, about to embark, rather blindly, on the next indicated stage. In a sense – though not in any formal sense, of course – it's going to be a 'graduate school' for what I've learned, in this way of life. I'm simply following signals, knowing by their manner of occurrence that where they lead must be right for me. Witness my understanding of the cues:

In the season of the year when sprouting happens (that is, around early February) . . . and directly proceeding from the recently ended stage ("directly" because it is something for which I qualify by having been a fulltime student) . . . a work-exchange program with Britain came to my attention (i.e., the prompt *crossed my path*, I wasn't chasing it). The final 'red carpet' touch is that the arrangements fell easily into place; there were no resistances to overcome.

So ... for the modest price of $96 to join the program, a one-way plane ticket ($299), and a passport ($42), I'll be off and away to six months of residency in England, starting in

September, with the 'blue card' privilege of holding a job there for that length of time.

I have no idea where, at what, or even *if* I'll obtain a job for that brief period, but the auspices are right and I'm willing to trust the situation. My funding, as it is shaping up, will be about $2500 plus my $391 monthly stipend from Social Security. Not much on which to predicate a year or more abroad, but that's exactly what I'm envisioning — six months in Britain and another six 'at large' on the continent, maybe longer . . . the most ambitious journey I have ever essayed.

Fresh out of School ... at 63

*Preparing, now, for a footloose journey abroad with
the prospect of hitch-hiking in foreign lands, I realized
that I was five years out of practice — not a good thing
at the somewhat critical age of 63. Taking advantage of
a commitment made to do a California workshop in the
spring of '90, I hit on the brilliant idea of making a hitch-
hike run of it from Seattle. This tale of the preliminary
adventure was incorporated into the book I later wrote
about the whole European journey: Innocence Abroad.*

Maybe it's the maverick in me that likes hitch-hiking, for
it certainly isn't an easy way to travel. Even though I
enjoy it, it begins always with discomfort — the sheer shock
of standing out on the road, a public spectacle, absorbing the
puzzled or judgemental gaze of every passing motorist. An
exercise in humility, confronting my pretensions . . . as well as
the parade of them coming by. And then there is impatience to
deal with, the vexatiously recurrent fear that no one will ever
stop. It vanishes in an instant, of course, when someone does . . .
and someone always does.

So I knew what to expect as I positioned myself at a
southbound freeway access on a mid-July morning, in Seattle's
University District. I propped my pack in a clearly visible
spot and held up a "Portland" sign, taking center-stage in a
drama about to open, playing a role that was only momentarily
uncomfortable. The day was as bright as July can be; and the

excitement, the pregnant tension of the open road, provided the adrenalin to pull me quickly into the spirit of adventure.

Hitching out of a large city means putting up with a thundering parade of mainly local traffic. Many hitch-hikers will sit tight, waiting for the long one even if it takes all morning. But riding is better than waiting, and I tend to trust the rightness of whatever comes along. It took about forty-five minutes for my ride to arrive, a mobile plumbing-repair shop that was hardly going anywhere near Portland, but the driver flashed a broad grin and just said, "Hop in!"

We were barely underway, moving into the stream of traffic, when my sign caught his eye again. "Oh, Oregon!" he exclaimed, "...Damn, what was I thinking of?"

He never quite explained that, but I gathered that he meant to go some other direction. Instead, he continued on down the freeway, telling me that he'd get me to another good hitching spot even though it took him far out of his way — like ten miles! It was a strange but seemingly auspicious start.

Where he let me off, another car pulled over so quickly that I had to grab my gear and run for it. This was a young fellow on his way to work, who took me another ten miles down the freeway. I was actually making progress — fitfully, like a sputtering engine that hadn't been run in a long while.

It was a lightly used access road I had to settle for, this time, and a much longer wait. It took about an hour before a classy Buick pulled over, driven by a tawny young airline stewardess. It's a bit unusual for me to be picked up by a good-looking woman driving alone, though it happens now and then. But climbing in, I spotted a substantial trickle of water running out from under the front of the car, which suggested a radiator problem.

Sure enough, it was boiling over, and we carefully released the pressure. But it was only a temporary fix, and there were no service facilities at hand. We limped into the freeway flow, rolling slowly along to the next exit, where we came directly upon a radiator repair shop as if it had been part of a planned scenario.

The thermostat had gone out, so it hadn't triggered either the cooling fan or the dashboard signal — that was the entire problem. A hurried patch was made to keep the fan going and let my anxious driver finish her trip; she could take care of it properly later on. In much easier spirits, now, she talked about her job and her hopes of going back to school, and I learned a bit about what the world of an airline stewardess is like. She dropped me off at a small town near Olympia, where the traffic was slow but sufficient, and the surroundings decidedly more peaceful than where my day began.

I reflected on the satisfying ride as I waited there for another. Hitch-hiking makes instant friendships – Christina was her name, a full-blooded Skykomish Indian – but it ends them just as quickly. Still, it left me with a warm glow, for had I not alerted Chris to her problem, she might have had a far more serious one on the freeway. It was her decision to stop and pick me up that protected her from it. Yet, there was something more to it. I wouldn't have been there had not the previous events on my journey been just as they were: the happenings we call 'pure chance' taking me precisely to where she would find me!

I've watched that sort of thing so many times on the road: chance events linking in an undeniably fruitful way. Maybe it is happening all the time, but hitch-hiking highlights it, for it is one of the few activities – indeed, they are rare today – that deliberately court the world of chance in daily life. To let go of control is not an easy thing to do, but it seems the most effective way for bringing Providence into view.

By four in the afternoon, two further rides had taken me into Portland and it seemed enough distance for a day's travel: 175 miles in six hours. I had friends in this city and could be sure of a night's shelter somewhere. First, however, I had to find someplace to freshen-up and get my bearings. Portland is the West Coast city I am least familiar with.

The journey thus far had given me little reason to doubt my readiness for it. I was tired, yes, but the day had turned hot and I had a larger pack than I was used to. Not at all large by backpacking standards, only about thirty pounds, but my highway travel was once done with little more than a daypack and sleeping bag.

I was also wearing heavier shoes than I liked — a pair of Rockports I was still breaking in. Pack and shoes suddenly teamed-up to topple me as I trudged wearily through Portland's riverfront section. My foot caught the edge of a curb, and down I went, the momentum of the pack pitching me into a full sprawl. It was more embarrassing than damaging, but I had a gash in my pants leg and a bad bruise under it. I wondered, as I band-aided the knee, if I was too far past my prime for this sort of thing. But a cup of tea lifted my spirits while I sorted over the prospects for Portland hospitality.

It was perhaps ten years since I had last seen Joan Lorenz — when I lived briefly near Monterey, where she and husband Roger partnered at a local alternative paper unforgettably called The Nose. She greeted me now with enthusiasm and not the least surprise at my road-weary condition, for Joan knew the ways of my life. A hot shower was offered for my aches and exhaustion, and for my hunger a cold summer meal; and then we had lots of catching-up to do — as much as could be done in one evening, for I wanted to be on my way again, next morning, to maintain the pace.

The second day was a punishing one. It got hot early, and I was stuck at an inner-city freeway access until just before noon. The ride that finally came took me barely out beyond the city limit. I was grateful. But this spot proved even worse! After two more useless hours, I started walking up the freeway — partly in disgusted need for a change of scenery, and partly to reach a more promising location. The walk was a mixed experience: sweaty in the blazing afternoon sun, but peaceful in the surround of Chopin and Vivaldi coming in on my radio, all else shut out by ear plugs. Three long miles I walked up the highway, ignoring the mad traffic alongside of me.

Walking into the sun, I switched from my usual narrow-brim hat to a visored one, which just happened to have military-style camouflage coloring, and I suspect it may have flagged my next ride. The fellow who pulled over for me as I was nearing the crest of a hill was a gung-ho patriot sort, a rancher from Idaho in a big whining pickup with a rifle slung against its back window. He said he was headed for Eugene, a good hundred miles down the state, and it looked like the fates had finally clicked-in for me. As we hummed along the highway, he told me how he had started his ranch from scratch and made it on his own, in the best American tradition. He began it as a personal tale, but I had the distinct impression it turned into a sermon. He all but spelled the message out, "Lift yourself up, man, set your sights as I did..."

About twenty miles along our way, he turned to me with a 'good buddy' look and suggested we stop for a drink; and that was my undoing. Without thinking of the implications, I innocently allowed as how I could certainly go for a cold Coke in this heat. He looked at me rather oddly, at that, and when we pulled into the next town he suddenly remembered some business he had there. He left me at a refreshment stand . . . after first buying me a Coke, and nothing at all for himself.

So there I was, well into a scorching afternoon, five hours on the road and not yet forty miles out of Portland. It was shaping up as a true test of my taste for this sort of adventure. Yet, there was nothing for me to do but go on with it.

It was a rather sad looking rural access road, this time — I wondered if it had any traffic at all, or if I'd only be walking in the hot sun again. But just as I started into it a freeway-bound pickup came flying by, and I barely had time to fling my thumb up, to make my needs known. A cloud of dust practically hid its sudden stop. But there was no room for me. Three Spanish-speaking crop hands filled every inch of cab space; all I could understand was their waving motion toward the open truck. They barely gave me time to clamber in, and lurched away at the same breakneck speed.

Except for the circumstance that I found myself nestled among big duffel bags, which proved to be comfortable riding cushions, I had every reason to suppose it was another short ride that would turn off at some local farm road. But it didn't. On they went . . . and on, and on. It was a wonderful ride, the finest sort that a hitch-hiker can get: I was stretched full length, feet forward, my head against those duffels, the wind rushing my hair and offsetting the sun's heat, and miles were going by as swiftly as the trees at roadside that rose sheer into the blue, from my truckbed perspective. We went past Eugene, past Cottage Grove, past Roseburg, on into the mountains hardly pausing to shift gears. I began to wonder if they were going clear to Mexico!

Deep in the mountains somewhere between Roseburg and Grants Pass, they turned off on a barren minor road, making some wild motions at me through the cab's rear window. Since they hardly slowed for it, I had no choice but to go along. We soon reached a tiny store and gas pump, where I could see they had arrived among friends. It was like a way-station on some covert underground railway; or more to the point, a pit stop in a high-rolling trucker's derby. They gassed-up, sat down to talk and eat awhile with other swarthy bracero-types, and I found a moment to get in some largely finger-pointing map talk with one of them — to discover that they were headed for Redding, halfway into northern California!

Well, an open pickup and the wind in your hair can be great sport in the sunshine, but it's miserable at night. And right now, the sun was about to be nibbled by the crest of the surrounding high line of hills. I had friends on either side of the state line, and I figured I'd just see how far daylight would take me.

They slowed a bit when the journey resumed. But evening came on rapidly and I was beginning to wonder if I'd be able to see where to hop off — and whether they'd stop the truck within walking distance, for me to do it. We came to the little town of Phoenix, where my Oregon friends lived, but it was behind us before I could even decide if I wanted to get off there. Hornbrook was now the place to look for, just across the state line; but my only memory of the place was a barren crossroad — long before the time of freeways. And it would soon be too dark to make out anything at all.

While I was turning these imponderables over, huddled against the now chill headwind, we suddenly slowed. I looked ahead to see the bright and blinking lights of California's agricultural inspection station, an enforced brief halt that I had forgotten all about. I realized instantly that it was exactly what I wanted.

"Adios amigos! Muchas gracias," I tossed off my entire grasp of the vernacular, waving them on their way as I let out a deep sigh of satisfaction . . . with the ride, with myself, with the whole day's irregular course of events. California, here I was! — in the sort of turnaround finale that's only possible in hitch-hiking, where chance lurks with every next car coming down the pike, and things somehow always work out.

Louis Durham, in his country seclusion at Hornbrook, was only a phone call away — and quite surprised that I was at the other end of it and close enough to be picked up. Once more I was closing a gap of many years. Lou had been an administrative minister at San Francisco's Glide Memorial Church during their wild and wooly '60s, and the prime organizing energy behind a pioneering middle-age, middle-class shared living situation, as well as other alternative developments of those years.

Again, it was only a one-night stay. I was feeling stronger, thanks no doubt to the day's fast finish, and wanted to get right on with it. I had no way of knowing it yet, but my instincts were right on target . . . I was tracking a piece of good fortune that had yet to show itself and I couldn't afford to be late.

I knew exactly where I was going the next day: to Red Bluff, 170 miles downstate. It called for just one good ride, and I got it quite easily at the border inspection station where all southbound cars have to stop. I even scored an air-conditioned vehicle, a stroke of first-rate luck since we were headed into California's hot Central Valley where the day's temperature was going to crest above 100 degrees.

My driver, this time, was a real estate appraiser from the Seattle area going to Sacramento for a family funeral. We had some stimulating conversation on a variety of topics for most of the two and a half hours that it took to reach Red Bluff, and he stopped there for a bite of lunch with me before resuming the journey alone. But I almost had second thoughts about letting him go on without me, when we stepped out of the car into a virtual furnace. I have friends with well-cooled homes in

Sacramento. But I knew I had to reconnect, here in Red Bluff, with Hal Howard. We had been housemates for three years in Berkeley, and had known and worked with each other since the early 1970s. I hadn't seen Hal since I settled in Seattle, and it was too long overdue.

This time, I would have stayed longer than one night . . . but here, it turned out, was the one place that I couldn't. Hal happened to be the only one along the route who knew I was coming, though he didn't know exactly when I'd show up. The day before I got there, he received a call from a mutual Berkeley friend, Yana Parker, who asked if he'd care to house-sit for a couple weeks. He didn't want to, himself, but he was quite sure that I would! I phoned Yana at once to confirm the arrangement, and it was so close to her departure time that I couldn't even hitch the rest of the way, but had to grab a bus into the city the next morning.

Yana's two weeks away were perfect for my own purposes. I hadn't made any prior plans for where I'd stay, in that period, simply because there are so many Bay Area friends to see when I am there, that I just assume I'll find a new host every few days. But this was perfection, for it gave me a central 'home' while I was there. The gift also included use of Yana's small Honda, providing all the mobility I might want. Even more, it gave me a telephone-response machine, a Macintosh with laser printer on which to finish my prep for the workshop next on my agenda, and a shy little cat to look after me when the day's activity was done.

Sometimes, in those twilight moments before drifting off to sleep, I find myself counting not sheep, nor blessings, but the amazing string of 'if's that have to fall into proper place for such impossible instances of Providence to materialize. *If*, in that last moment of my last ride, I had decided to go on to Sacramento...

If I hadn't soured that Idaho rancher exactly in time to catch those three California-bound braceros... *If* I had neglected to let Hal know I was coming, or *if* he just hadn't thought of me when Yana called... It is truly mind-boggling.

Yana Parker, in the days when we saw more of each other, used to put out a lively little communal newsletter that circulated like a grapevine – which is what it was called – among a good many of the collective-living houses in the Bay Area. The timing of her two weeks away meshed so perfectly with my own that on the very day she returned I was off and away to the south toward Monterey, and the Asilomar site of my workshop.

There's really not much to say about the workshop that belongs in this book. The subject of it was a fascination of mine that has deepened over the years: the seasonal cycle and its influence on consciousness and our reality. It was well-received, and shortly afterward I made my swift way back to Seattle by an inexpensive overnight bus called the Green Tortoise. I could not afford to dally, for only two weeks remained in which to finalize every last detail before taking off on the greatest adventure of my not-exactly-humdrum life.

On the whole, I was quite satisfied with the roadtrip. People who should know had told me that hitch-hiking is no longer as easy as it used to be, but the magic of my own had been quite as good as ever. I was gratified that I still had the energy for that sort of travel, and my stamina seemed remarkable for 63 years of a non-athletic life. If I pay attention to where I plant my big feet, I should have no future trouble at all.

Hitching Abroad

In the summer of 1991, my trust in the providence of the open road and that particular way of life reached its zenith in a free-and-easy jaunt through Europe, both East and West. I was 64 now, and traveling alone in territory where I knew practically no one, with no foreign language facility at my disposal. Doing it, also, with funds too minimal for overnight shelter in hotel rooms anywhere but in the most economically depressed parts of eastern Europe.

What I relied on, instead, was a no-cost hosting network of people called Servas that I had taken a year's membership in. But unable to plan ahead with the assurance of a travel itinerary, I was reduced to contacting these good folks as I went, when and where I happened to turn up. So I could never know, for sure, with whom I might be staying, wherever the fortunes of vagabond travel found me each night. I was out on a limb about as far as I could let myself go.

It was only partially a hitch-hiking journey, as I availed myself of the most convenient – and of course, affordable – style of travel at hand. But it included hitch-hiking segments in Great Britain, France, Netherlands, Germany, Poland, Austria and Greece — some of those all too briefly. But in a certain sense – the hitch-hiking way of life, absorbed from so many years on the road at home – I could easily say that I was hitch-hiking all the way.

I wrote a book on the whole experience, spanning 19 months that included bracketing winters of residence in London and on the Greek isle of Lesbos. It's called *Innocence Abroad*, and I've culled three more tales from that book – in addition to the previous chapter – for your enjoyment.

The first of these took place in Scotland: in a day's time, I went from a high point of my U.K. circuit to a major crisis of confidence in my ability to carry the whole adventure through. This is how it got resolved — by an unexpected instance of providential grace, of course.

The next two tales are on the Continent proper — one in Poland, the other in Germany. Each presents a different display of how a hitch-hiker's providence functions on the open road, often in ways so entirely without precedent, or likelihood of happening, that they can truly blow your mind (or what is left of it by the time you've come this far).

If these tales prompt you to seek the full book, you'll find further details on it at the end of this one. Meanwhile, enjoy . . .

Episode 10.1

Quest and Crisis in Scotland

I walked out of Conwy across one of the twin bridges that span the Afon River, and a half-mile onward to a vehicle roundabout — a traffic circle hub for several intersecting roads. It held such a tight weave of Saturday traffic that the inner ring wasn't moving at all, the outer ring not much better. I found the spin-off that went east toward England and stood there — more conspicuous than I wanted to be in the circumstances. A hitch-hiker can't very well be retreative about his activity, but being the only new thing for several hundred stalled drivers to put their eyeballs on was not what I needed.

But my rescue was not long in coming: two of the most attractive young women, I daresay, that I have ever received a ride with, and we were into almost instant conversation — about my journey, my way of life, and some of their perspectives on life that reflected a good deal of depth. It was a half-hour of thorough enjoyment, until they stopped at a roadside restaurant for a bit of lunch. I was invited to join, but I could see at once that it was beyond my means so I simply said I'd rather not delay my travels, and would hitch on from there. They said they'd pick me up again if I should still be there after lunch.

I must have stood there with my thumb out, ineffectually, for nearly an hour. Just as they emerged and got into their car, with a look and a wave in my direction, some damn fool driver coming out of the parking lot ahead of them stopped for me! It was one of those awful slow-motion, fast-action moments: he opening his side-door, me standing there in momentary indecision about how to handle it, and the young women cheerfully waving as they went around the whole tableau and out onto the highway. I think it was the only time in my hitch-hiking life that I ever experienced deep disappointment on getting a ride after an hour's wait.

I wasn't much for conversation with the poor fellow, and he didn't take me very far, perhaps fifteen miles. I didn't even give him a very cheery farewell. He surely thought me the most ungrateful wretch he'd ever picked up — never knowing why.

I got over it by the time my next ride came along, a middle-aged couple who said they stopped because of the American flag pinned to my pack. I often wondered at the ratio of people who picked me up because of it, to those who let me stand because of it. This driver went out of his way to take me into Chester, the region's largest town and my day's target. Chester would be my springboard toward Scotland. But the place was a surprise I hadn't expected: a remarkably picturesque town center with a wonderful array of half-timbered old structures, their upper stories over-hanging the sidewalks in a cozy, sheltering way, projecting a perfect traditional image of Elizabethan England.

But here, alas, I hit a roadblock on the Servas list. With a dozen numbers to call, I couldn't make a good connection with anyone. I waited a half-hour and made a second round of calls to those who simply hadn't answered, and — bingo! I turned up a host in the neighboring town of Mickle Trafford. It took nearly another hour, in the deepening twilight, to get out there, and once more I found myself provided with an unusually restful situation, my third such in a row. The gods were taking better care of me than I was of myself.

David and Vanessa were a compelling mid-50s couple in many respects. He was, by persuasion, a former Tory councilman for the region. And by profession, a dairy farmer herding 125 head of cattle — though one would never suspect it from the secluded appearance of his country property, nestled behind rows of screening hedge in an area that seemed more suburban than rural. He was also one of the most challenging and wily – I am tempted to say deadly – conversationalists I have ever encountered. David loved the verbal duel and he was a master at it. I had to be really on my toes to stay abreast of him in a joust, let alone to best him at it, which I never succeeded in doing. I could hardly help but gain some respect for his politically conservative convictions.

Vanessa, for her part, was a more companionable sort of conversationalist, with empathy the keynote of her style, able to convey instant while yet sincere friendship — a difficult combination. She also baked a thief-tempting nut bread. Their home was expansive, though not ostentatious, but the upstairs room they put me in seemed the combined size of every bedroom I'd had, all week long. The great double bed hardly made a dent in its generous space. Sunday morning in that room was like a moment of eternity, and I spent an hour in bed browsing a century-old copy of Mrs. Beeton's Household Hints, a staple of Victorian Britain, with everything from recipes to advice for the lovelorn. One memorable passage described the best, or maybe the oldest, method for tenderizing a flank of beef: place it under the saddle of your trotter before his morning run.

I had every good reason to idle all of Sunday away, there, but my travels had acquired a momentum of their own. I was obsessed with making the most of every day, and Liverpool was close enough for a side-trip from Mickle Trafford. I did it on Sunday – to find nothing there worth the effort – in disregard of the exhaustion slowly piling up in me. But I wasn't really aware of that yet. I had now come through two weeks on the road, with no evident problem except the on-again/off-again VISA card — and it had just worked for me in Chester. My expenses were slightly over budget, but not enough to worry about. Everything seemed to indicate that I was doing fine.

Vanessa packed some nutbread and a banana for me on Monday, and then I went north like a shot: took a bus out beyond the Liverpool-Manchester axis, to a motorway entrance, and very quickly got a ride with a Scottish businessman who drove me clear through to Carlisle, more than 100 miles and just shy of the border, a substantial distance in Britain, where the entire variegated 'island' is incredibly packed into a land mass hardly more than half the size of California's. He offered to take me all the way to Glasgow, but I was intent on a certain mission now, a quest that would take me instead on a slant toward Edinburgh.

I had, in fact, intended Carlisle as the day's destination, never imagining I would make it by noon. It was perfect, though; we had come through a violent storm that was behind me now, and the day invited a continuance right on toward Hawick, the village I wanted next to reach. But it was on a secondary road, and instead of resuming the hitch-hike it seemed wise to consider regional transit from Carlisle.

Walking the mile from the motorway into town with that in mind, I encountered a wonderful old Scot with a r-r-r-rich Harry Lauder voice (does anyone still remember Harry Lauder's

Scottish burr?), who seemed absolutely delighted at the sight of me, near to bursting with uncontainable joy. He caught me poring over my map at a street corner and made a one-man welcoming committee of himself. I thought, later, I might easily have cajoled a night's shelter of him had I been inclined to stay in Carlisle, but the mid-day urge to move on was too strong.

I had known I was headed for Hawick – which is pronounced 'Hoyick' – long before I knew I'd even make the journey. It was the first of three unique quests that would provide a periodic bit of investigative focus to my otherwise haphazard travels. Detective adventures of the 'needle in a haystack' sort — although I didn't yet realize that the one in Hawick was anything more than the simple fulfillment of a promise to a friend, with no anticipated complications.

Jim Hall is an elderly fellow I came to know during my first year of settlement in Seattle. He's something of a recluse, gifted with a sharp and perceptive mind that nourishes a critical irascibility toward the foibles of society, which probably accounts for the ageless inner vitality that belies his now ninety years. He grew up in Liverpool and came to America in his youth, leaving behind a sister who for many years had been living in Hawick. I had given Jim my assurance that if I went anywhere near there I would pay her a visit for him. That was the mere extent of it . . . until I got to Hawick.

The bus from Carlisle went through some of the most idyllic meadow country I had yet encountered: rich green rolling hills with just the right measure of scattered oak, an occasional stream, yet hardly any sign of habitation, and all of it gleaming in the freshness of recent rainfall. The countryside was so entrancing, so pristine, that it was almost a shock to burst suddenly into the rather substantial town of Hawick. The address that Jim had given me for Jean Hyslop had led me to expect a small village, for it was only the name of a road, Buccleuch, with no house number. I was surprised and dismayed, then, to learn that Buccleuch was a long and prominent street in town with numbered housing to its outer extremity.

So it became a quest. But not before I had first checked the telephone directory to discover more than a dozen Hyslops listed, none of them Jean or J, and none of them on Buccleuch. The clock said 4:30 and I figured a quick check with some county office would be the most productive course of action. But when I reached the Town Hall it had already shut down for the day. With no other bright idea, I asked an available cleaning woman if she had any thoughts of how to pursue this search. She suggested I check with the post office up the street.

On my way to it, rushing lest I get there also too late, I went past a window that said Town Council, and someone was just emerging and locking the door. I put my problem immediately to him, and he said I should not go to the main post office but to the branch of it that was right at the head of Buccleuch, back in the other direction. I turned back immediately and headed for it, almost at a trot, pack and all. It was still open when I got there . . . but the clerk was not at all familiar with Jean's name. She suggested I try the music store about halfway down the first block of Buccleuch, saying the proprietor had been on the street a long time and probably knew everybody on it.

The music shop man, after thinking a bit, couldn't recall any Jean Hyslop, either. I prodded him with the possibility that she might be in the care of younger folk, and he recalled an elderly woman with a young couple at "that house over there with the stairs jutting out," a bit further down the road. But when I asked the young couple there, they just shook their heads and suggested I try at the antique shop, a few doors back. This was becoming absurd, by now, but having no other trail I continued with it.

The folks in the antique shop thought they'd seen several elderly people living in an adjoining courtyard. I went in there and at once ran into a fellow in overalls who wanted to know what I was looking for. I put the story to him, in its accumulating detail, and he pondered awhile and wondered if it might be an elderly woman he knew as Mrs. Jean Lennox, who used to live there and whose name had been changed by a recent marriage. She now lived up the hill, he told me, off to the side of Buccleuch Road, at a place called St. Margaret's Retirement Home. It all seemed unlikely but I went off up the hill to check it out.

The attendant who answered the door didn't know a Jean by either name, but thought I should try across the way, at the Buccleuch Retirement House. This seemed immediately promising, for it could account for Jim's failure to provide a number — even if it wasn't actually on Buccleuch Road. But the names brought no flash of recognition here, either. Then the woman at the door had a sudden thought and asked me to wait a minute. She returned a few moments later with a gleam in her eye, saying she'd found what I was looking for. One of her chair-bound tenants, it seemed, had a visitor that very afternoon, who turned out to be . . . Jean Hyslop! I was given an address for the Balgownie Retirement House, some distance out on Buccleuch Road.

I went out there immediately — and sure enough, it was Jim's sister. A frail wisp of a woman for whom I had to keep the conversation narrowly focused, she was quite amazed and charmed, that a friend of brother Jim from faraway Seattle should seek her out, here. And I, of course, was still dizzy from the trail of serendipity that had made absolutely no rational sense, yet had put me on Jean's doorstep within 90 minutes of when the search was started. We had an hour-long visit over tea and cookies, before I took my leave for fear of exhausting her.

I don't know how many angels were involved in that run of referrals. Any one of them could have stopped the trail cold by not sending me on to the next. But one, at least, was certainly an angel: the man in the overalls, for he was not anyone I was specifically referred to, and he was the one who intervened to direct me off Buccleuch Road, and toward – for all I could know – perhaps Jean's only friend in town.

But it was time for the journey's reckoning to begin.

I had harbored the hope that in locating Jean I might also find a place of lodging for the night, for there was neither a host nor hostel anywhere near Hawick. It was clear, though, that I'd receive no invitation to pass the night in a retirement home. The sensible choice at this point would have been a B & B, and I could have stretched for the $20 that one would have cost me here. Even though the skies were clear, it was cold, cold, cold . . . and I was weary, weary, weary. But I was fixated on budget concerns and I had already overspent, this day, with bus rides at both ends of my run. Weary and cold, or not, it was going to be a night spent out in the rough.

In the lingering daylight of this northern latitude, I had time enough to survey the town, to find the most likely spot that would keep me dry, warm, and unseen. So I put away my victorious quest and got down to the nitty-gritty of trudging from one end of town to the other. Staggering would be more like it, for I took another one of those stumbling falls on a raised bit of sidewalk, just as I had – in another lifetime, it seemed – in Portland. I was up before a count of ten, but I was clearly on my last legs. Clear to me now, not then.

I found my spot in the shelter of a grandstand on an open, accessible athletic field — so open that I had to wait until full darkness to be sure no one would spot me. One can never be too careful about bedding down in the midst of a town. Even at 10:30, I felt the need to take an evasive route to avoid people in parked cars — perhaps only young lovers who wouldn't have noticed, but a lurking stranger is the target of every suspicion. It must have been near midnight before I was securely settled, and warm enough in my down bag to drift off to that sweet harbor of rejuvenation.

And then some internal devil snapped me out of my sleep shortly after four in the morning, and I couldn't reclaim it. I lay there until daybreak watching the bright morning stars, and then worked as fast as possible to get my gear together in order to stay warm. But it was at least another shivering hour before any place in town serving hot coffee was open.

By the time I was underway again, beneath a mercifully warm sun in a cloudless sky, I knew I wasn't feeling my usual morning charge of energy. I primed the pump again with a full breakfast at a roadside cafe, but that didn't help either. It was nothing I could put my finger on, just 'the blahs.' Two rides took me the forty miles to Edinburgh, a city that would have cheered and fascinated me on any other day, but not this one. I moped around a park in the heart of town, not even feeling like calling a host, but I knew I must. It would mean I'd have to be sociable, and certainly no burden, and the prospect had all the appeal of a ride on a roller coaster.

But sitting in the park offered no relief, either. The city seemed intolerably noisy. By mid-afternoon the sunlight, challenged by a growing swarm of clouds, had decided to quit its job and the air was turning chill again. I hadn't even any interest in a giant booksale underway near the park — which verified that I was in pretty bad shape.

So I went to the phone, only to encounter the ultimate disaster: a solid wall of rejection. Even calling the unanswered numbers an hour later, as in Chester, brought no result. It was after 6:30 now, and I considered my options. I could take a train for Glasgow and another cluster of possible hosts, an hour away — but that was a gamble, and the time and energy drain of it didn't appeal to me. Or I could try the Edinburgh youth hostel — and pay eleven dollars for a dorm bed. Or try the two suburban hosts on the list, which I had avoided up to now. I called one in the town of Dunfermline, fifteen miles north, and she answered! I had a bit of difficulty with her thick Scotch burr, but I was fairly sure I heard her say that she was no longer a Servas host. And then, perhaps sensing my agony, she said I could come over anyway.

It was quite exactly the place I needed in that moment. Kathleen, a soft-spoken redhead with an easy smile that resided more in her eyes than anywhere else on her features, was an independent computer analyst, and as easy-going on social protocol as any host I'd had. She understood my situation immediately and prepared an instantly therapeutic bowl of hot soup, and then told me that I could remain there the entire next day by myself while she took care of business elsewhere. I curled up shortly afterward and slept about ten hours that night.

In the morning I was completely useless. Not a grain of energy, and my whole body ached. The prospect of only a day here was frightening when I let myself dwell on it. I knew better, of course — Kathleen would let me stay on if I had to. But I was faced with a real concern that I could not dodge. If this is what happens to me after two weeks on the road, what is it telling me about the rest of my journey? Never mind Europe, what about the remaining three weeks in Britain?

In the purest turn of fate, or let us say that by the gift of the gods, Kathleen happened to have a copy of the *I Ching* among the books on her shelves. I'm not entirely sure, but it could well have been the first copy I had seen since I arrived in Britain. For those not familiar with the book, it's an ancient Chinese oracle system. It's much more than that, but this is not the place for a detailing. The *I Ching* had been my chief source of guidance for many years in California, and while I don't fully understand the working of it (no one really does), I have seen enough of its potency and reliability to have the highest respect for it.

The question that confronted me now, about the wisdom of continuing this journey, was precisely the sort of question for which the *I Ching* is best used. Which is to say, merely, that I was on the fence with it. I was teetering between yes and no, and could accept either determination — but needed some sureness of making the best choice. By some strange and marvelous alchemy incredible to our rational ways, the *I Ching* is somehow able to reflect back to us what we already know at some level, but don't know that we know, because of all the static thrown up by the reasoning mind. It's as simple, and as complex, as that.

I covered both sides of the matter, asking the question in a format that is only for those with a well-honed feeling for the *I Ching*: Should I persevere, or call it off? Its response, in the form of a text reading, affirmed my journey and provided some perspective on why I had been tripped-up by this sudden physical agony. For the first time, I saw how insistently and insensitively I had been pushing myself to the limit of physical endurance. It was a healthy corrective, and I resolved to listen more closely thereafter to the cues I had been virtually ignoring.

It was a critical moment for the summer that was taking shape for me. On the turn of a coin – the method employed in consulting the *I Ching* – I would have called off the whole adventure. But the moment was magical, along with my 'chance fortune' of having reached Kathleen's, where the trusty oracle was available. And Kathleen, of course, ranks as a full-fledged angel, for me. The crisis was successfully navigated.

Episode 10.2

Touring Poland with my German Chauffeur

E verything gets distorted when the denominations on your paper money run to five figures. I cashed twenty deutschemarks in the little office doing an exchange business at the Polish border and received 125,000 zlotys. I had no idea, yet, what this sort of money would buy, but I was at once uncomfortable with such high-figure currency and fumbled for words to explain that I wanted smaller bills. The bemused woman took back one of the 10,000 zloty notes and gave me a handful of 500s. I'm sure she thought me simple-minded as I smiled my thank-you, for each one of these had less value than a nickel! I was just a little slow to connect the fact that my entire exchange didn't amount to $11.

I walked south out of town alongside the river levee on a quiet, tree-shaded road – an easy four-miles, hardly disturbed by vehicle traffic – to the Berlin-Warsaw highway. Couples and small family groups strolled by with buckets of berries from a small farmer's market and bazaar, just off the roadway in a grove of trees. I looked briefly in on it, and was boggled by prices like

15,000 zlotys per pound. I finally bought a big hunk of goat cheese for 7,875 zlotys (sixty-eight cents), to nibble on my way.

It must have been past noon when I reached the highway, a divided high-speed strip, two lanes on either side. I paused on the overpass to contemplate the idling line of huge trucks patiently waiting on their border clearance into Germany. In the other direction only an occasional car zipped by, and I could see the prospect of a long wait ahead of me. But the mid-day sun wasn't oppressive; I had only my own impatience to contend with.

I was merely standing there absorbed in these ruminations, gazing down at the scene, when suddenly a big gray sedan was alongside of me, its driver speaking English with a slight accent. He asked where I was going and if I wanted a ride! There are times when I can't quite believe my own life.

He was German, out to sample the Polish countryside, he said, for maybe a day or two, not even sure of where he'd be going. It was fine with me — neither was I. His name was Albert: mid-30's, short, bespectacled, with curly dark hair fringing a premature baldness — the entire aspect lending a cerebral appearance, which was not misleading. Albert had an inquiring mind interested in everything, though nothing very deeply. In fact, a dispassionate objectivity seemed to be his only passion. He evidenced remarkably little personal involvement with anything he talked about.

We discovered very quickly, though, something in common besides this perfect mutual timing for a visit into Poland. Albert was a semi-committed follower of Bhagwan Shree Rajneesh, who had recently died in Poona, India, after having outraged the good people of Oregon for several years and then been banished from further residence in the U.S. Albert had lived at the Poona Ashram for more than a year, until shortly before the charismatic

Bhagwan's death. For my part, I had stayed a month or two at the Oregon community, Rajneeshpuram, as a visiting outsider in the early 1980s, before the place was convulsed and destroyed by scandal. That unfortunate finale overshadowed a remarkable instance of communal development, with much more to its credit than is generally allowed in the wake of what ultimately came of it.

But they set their own fate in motion. A defining characteristic of those who were deeply involved in the Rajneesh experience was their inner circle attitude, grown from a conviction that they were more in touch with life's mysterious depth than the common herd — an elitism that was bound to alienate them from the rest of humanity. Albert had this quality. He skimmed the countryside quite insulated from it in his high-profile BMW, almost godlike in a bubble of self-elevation. We sped through towns that cried out for closer inspection, hardly stopping long enough for personal urgencies. It was a top quality highway across level country with virtually no traffic to slow us, and Albert – fresh from Germany's congested autobahns – took it at speeds that were foolish, if not foolhardy. From years of hitch-hiking, I've learned to accept whatever comes and stay cool. But had Albert asked, I was not enjoying it nearly as much as he seemed to be. But then again, I hadn't even had to raise a thumb; I could hardly complain.

We reached Poznan, a third of the way to Warsaw and the only sizable city on the route, just before four in the afternoon. This was as far as Albert had intended to go. But it was such a fine road, beyond all his expectations, that he was tempted, he said, to drive all the way to Warsaw. Not without a night to sleep on the question, however. He found a hotel to suit his taste and pocketbook — on neither of which I could concur. So we parted at that point, agreeing to meet there for breakfast.

In the possibility of a morning ride to Warsaw, I decided not to seek a Servas host and made my way instead to a youth hostel in a multi-use old school building. It was a hostel out of the Dark Ages. Sagging old cots with barely adequate bedding, shower stalls so filthy I decided against using one, no toilet paper . . . but it was cheap: $3.60 for the night. And private — an entire top-floor room to myself. Dormer windows looked out on a mid-city scene less imposing than that of Leipzig, but with the same sense of easy, quiet living — a simplicity sharply contrasting the haste and hustle of Berlin. Something about it, in fact – perhaps the entire lack of dazzle and show, and the streetcars down below – took me back again to the San Francisco of my youth. The narrow little trams, so crowded they appeared to have been built for children or pygmies, ran in tandem pairs and were tapered at each end, reminiscent of futuristic design in the 1930s.

Free of Albert, and with a few daylight hours left to explore my first Polish city, I set out walking and followed my instincts toward the center of town — a great market square. It was like stepping into a long-vanished age, for hardly a single visible structure could have been less than two-hundred years old. A turreted, vintage city hall, its pedigree indicated by an emblem and a date: 1555, occupied center stage in the square. Trailing to the rear of it, a string of marvelously narrow buildings of jumbled height and roof-line — a retinue, like an undisciplined line of soldiers following their leader in comic disarray. While around the perimeter, a phalanx of ancient structures stood in witness, like a sober gallery of judges, lending dignity to the jocular effect of the central scene.

Somewhere beyond the square I came to a massive, bulky church, clearly very old. It was plain and drab, huddled by equally unattractive buildings that had long ago crowded into its onetime grounds leaving no airspace whatever. I'd have gone on by, but the door was open and so I hazarded a quick look — and was struck, as if by an outpouring of choir song, by what I saw: an interior of carved and polished hardwood with sculpture everywhere, all in a color scheme of black with gold trim. My eyes went upward along massive marble pillars to artwork on the ceiling — pillars that appeared to be solid black marble all the way up, for I could detect no break in them, although their girth could not have been embraced by two men with outstretched arms. Interestingly, not a trace of stained glass could be seen. Yet, it took my breath away like no other cathedral I'd seen — and its drab exterior had given me not the slightest hint.

The next morning, slow in waking and unable to reach Albert by phone, I took a taxi for the several blocks to his hotel, unreasonably fearful of losing the possible ride to Warsaw. In my tourist-haste I got burned, paying more for that short ride than the night's lodging had cost. But I found Albert waiting, and my imprudent loss was offset when he bought me breakfast in the hotel. He even let me shower in his room before checking out.

We did some further local sightseeing before taking to the road again. I found a bookstore, and a beautifully illustrated volume on *Secesja* style, Poland's own version of France's *Art Nouveau*. It cost me $6.50, a fraction of its likely value in the States, were it even available there, and it suggested a fresh track for old pursuits that had been frustrated ever since I left England. Time and again on the continent I had walked into book shops from pure habit — pure useless habit, it had become, for all I saw was French, Belgian, Dutch and German texts. From now on, I would enjoy my old pastime in the universal language of art!

We made the 190-mile dash to Warsaw like Barney Oldfield wheeling it for a trophy. Such traffic as we encountered in this level farmland country moved at a snail's pace, probably set by the long, barrow-like horse-drawn wagons still in use here. More than once Albert had to brake sharply, exercising all the control he had, to avoid some vehicle changing lanes at thirty miles per hour — the poor peasant at the wheel hardly expecting anything like Albert on the road.

We got to Warsaw at three in the afternoon. Albert managed to find a tourist office where someone who spoke English was willing to make phone calls for us — to Servas hosts for me, and hotel possibilities for Albert. It required six tries before I finally made a connection on mine with a possible host: they were waiting for another traveler who was already two days late in arrival, and I took the opening on that edge of uncertainty. Albert had several leads he was anxious to check out, so we followed that route first and he took a room at the second stop. All of a sudden, then, he tired of being my chauffeur. He was quite weary, he said, and just wanted to get some rest, and could I please find my own way to the host I was headed for.

It's strange, how easily one gets accustomed to the ever-present utility and ease of an automobile. I felt momentarily angry with Albert for wanting his own life back! But I contained it and bid him a cheerful farewell — after all, he had taken me clear across Poland.

It took me a few moments to return to the headspace of the solitary traveler and grasp the responsibility of finding my way in this huge city. I had a poor excuse for a city map, picked up at the tourist office. It didn't even extend to where my host lived, which we had pin-pointed on Albert's larger map. But I knew that a bus along this boulevard went out there, and I knew the sort of intersection to watch for once I reached the vicinity.

Things, of course, never look like they're supposed to. I got off the bus too soon because I was afraid of getting off too late. But could I even be sure that I hadn't already done so? I was at a major intersection that was off my map, in an open area with good visibility, guessing that my destination should be not far ahead. I tried to make sure — if only I could find someone among the crowd at the bus stop who understood me. But one after another gave me an uncomprehending stare. This was the nightmare that had always haunted me: lost in Warsaw without a map, and nothing but blank looks for my every entreaty. I finally had to assume I must be right, and continue on down the main boulevard toward a row of condo-style high-rises in the middle distance.

I passed no one at all. It was very much like new suburban development areas at home, where nothing but automobiles are encountered. Finally, up ahead, a young woman came toward me. I paused as we passed, hesitantly asking whether she spoke any English.

"Sure do!" came the bright, smiling response. "Where y'from?"

An American! I could hardly trust my ears. It's not so rare to hear English spoken abroad, usually with German or Dutch accent, or else almost always British — but the distinctive sound of an American voice, in this remote Warsaw moment, was almost rapturous.

Not merely American, it turned out, but from my old San Francisco backyard: El Cerrito, California. She was in Warsaw on a student exchange for the summer. We stood and talked for awhile, and she confirmed that I was going in the right direction, probably to one of those very condos. Just as we turned toward our separate paths she tossed me a parting suggestion: "Go to Krakow — it's worth seeing."

My Warsaw hosts were Bogdan and Ewa, he an architect who worked at home and she an English teacher, completely fluent. Their condo apartment was a bit on the crowded side with two small children and all of Bogdan's work materials, but I was frankly surprised at their well-provisioned life, after all I had thus far seen in eastern Europe. The only thing in the kitchen that harked back to earlier times in my life was a table-affixed, hand-turned meat grinder. For all else, I could as easily have been in a modern middle-class American apartment. Bogdan was a book collector and they had somehow crammed more shelving space into that apartment than I'd have thought possible. But then the clever, efficient use of space is something Europeans have a talent for — from their long historical development of conservative land use for a steadily expanding population.

I gave myself all of Wednesday to explore Warsaw. The city was extraordinarily alive, bursting with energy and street sounds, an incredible tumult of people and activity in all directions. It felt like I had walked into a mass re-birthing underway, with none of the jaded, slick feeling of Berlin's Kurfurstendamm, but the freshness of something seeking its own form and style. Sidewalk stands selling everything from cassette tapes to kitchenware lined the streets. The only negative note was a massive instance of bulk architecture called the Culture Tower, a brooding reminder of recent history that dominates the city by its sheer, singular size. I suspect it dates from the Communist years, but whether so or earlier, it radiates the cold linearity of life dominated by ideology, and I'm sure the city would be lovelier and happier, and probably flower with more grace, if they tore it down.

Beyond the central area I discovered the oldest part of town, by the river Wisla; and near there a monumental tribute to the Warsaw Uprising of 1945, when the city was tragically betrayed by Soviet forces they had counted on to help oust the Nazis. It was one of the most awesome sculptural groupings I have ever seen: a larger than life assemblage of desperate figures in torment and violence, practically vibrating in their realism and intensity.

Ewa had spoken of a museum devoted to *Secesja* art in the town of Plock, sixty miles to the northwest. I bought a rail ticket that afternoon, figuring that an early Thursday start should let me visit the museum and then take an afternoon train from there to Wroclaw, on a direct line toward Prague. But when Bogdan pulled out his railroad schedules that evening, it proved impossible to put together an itinerary that wouldn't involve an overnight stay in Plock, plus other complications. So I dropped the whole idea, deciding instead to heed the advice of the young woman from El Cerrito. I'd take the Krakow express at 9:25 in the morning. Ewa wrote a note for me to present at the ticket counter requesting a ticket exchange.

At breakfast, Bogdan suddenly decided it was the moment to tell me all about the Warsaw Ghetto, the old Jewish quarter that the Nazis had flattened to rubble. It was 8:30 before I finally got on my way — time enough to just miss the bus that could have taken me to the train station in good time. I got the next bus . . . just in time to keep me on edge all the way into town. It took a route that was new to me. I lost sight of the landmark Culture Palace and lost my bearings in the maze of turns the bus took. It followed a long, roundabout route while time kept ticking away and I kept trying to figure out where I was. The whole plan seemed headed for disaster. I finally spotted the low, rectangular station facade just seven minutes before train time.

By then, it was too late to mess with the ticket counter line, so the problem assumed new dimensions. I had made a short hop in Holland without a ticket, but . . . a three-and-a-half hour express to Krakow? It was either take it without a ticket, or not at all. I got on and settled myself in a compartment with five others to await whatever should develop.

Mile after mile, no conductor appeared on the scene as we whizzed across the Polish flatlands and into rolling hills. I imagined the worst – getting thrown off the train – and figured I had better just act dumb . . . which wouldn't really be an act. We must have been halfway to Krakow before a conductor looked in and everyone reached for their ticket. Like some school kid with a note from home, I handed him the request that Ewa had written the night before. He studied it with a frown, then wrote something below and handed it back to me. Was that all? No. He brought forth a little book from an inner pocket and began making calculations, finally indicating that I must pay a 33,000 zloty fare plus a 5000 zloty penalty for boarding the train without a ticket. Total price for the 180-mile express to Krakow: $3.35.

Something about Krakow felt delightfully refreshing from the moment that I arrived. The usual fruit stands and diverse entrepreneurs surrounded the depot, and I had to fend off taxi drivers, one of whom insistently wanted to drive me to Auschwitz. I brushed him away, remembering what I'd said to Albert when he spoke of wanting to see the Holocaust death camps: "not now, and not ever." None of these things seemed unusually refreshing, but a certain atmosphere hovered in the air like the breath of a late spring morning, though we were well into summer.

My second phone call turned up a host. Mindful of the six calls it required in Warsaw, I told him earnestly that I'd even be comfortable sleeping on a floor. His indignation at the very suggestion rang loud and clear. "No guest in my house sleeps on the floor!"

This was Greg (short for Grzegorz) who lived just an easy walk from the station, on the second floor of an old six-unit frame building — the very place he'd been born, he would later tell me, forty-four years ago. The whole building had once belonged to his family before Communism took their ownership away. Greg wasn't sure that he'd ever get title to it again, for the old records had long ago been destroyed. He lived there now with a child, who was away, and his wife, Gorza — secretary for the local theater company, a sometimes actress and would-love-to-be taxicab dispatcher, who could sit for hours listening to their radio dialogue. Greg was a journalist, interpreter and also a local disc jockey. Together, they made one of the warmest, most engaging pairs that I encountered on my entire trail.

Part of Krakow's instant charm was surely due to the circumstance that it had come cleanly through the war — one of the few major cities that hadn't been damaged at all. In consequence, it had continued to age in a graceful fashion, never forced into that dispiriting mix of old and new that reveals, by glaring prominence, what can no longer be decently maintained. Yes, buildings still fall into aged disuse here, but they blend with the rest of the old city in an overall image of harmony. A fascinating array of ancient architecture lined the quaint and narrow streets, continually surprising me with picture-postcard scenes at each fresh turn. At one such, I walked right into one of the grandest open squares, easily, in all of central Europe.

Krakow's market square is so immense that an Alhambra-like structure, huge itself, nestles within it like a jewel set into a ring. Called the Cloth Hall, it's a football field long, rising several stories, yet it doesn't compromise the open feeling of the square as a whole, which incorporates other structures as well.

The effect of a town or market square on the life of a community, as I saw it time and again in Europe, in small towns and large cities, is so invigorating and so graceful at the same time that I can't help feeling profoundly sad for its absence in the cities of America. People invariably gravitate to such areas, which certainly expresses an inner need for their social function. It is nothing like a shopping mall, where the emphasis is on trade and parking space, not community. The open square motif is to be found only one place in America: on its great University campuses; but in civic life, in this land of seemingly endless land, we are too overwhelmed by property values to indulge in anything so profitless as open space.

I managed to see a good deal of Krakow during my two days there, but – as with few other cities – it seemed impossible to get enough. On my second day, I joined Gorza at the end of her workday, and she took me on a tour of the 100-year-old theater and opera house, showing me parts of the building that few ever see. The onetime dressing room of their oldest and most revered actor, Ludwick Solski, has been kept intact, its walls covered by testimonials and mementos, since his death at age 99 in the mid-1950s.

Then I took Gorza to see a discovery I had made, myself, that day. In the dark corridor to an inner court, in one of the many old Krakow apartment buildings, I found a remnant of *Secesja* building art: a lovely panel of red poppies in stained and leaded glass, dirtied but intact above the interior portal. She had seen it before, but we stood and admired it for the time it took our eyes to adjust to the darkened passage. Going out, then, into the sudden bright light of the street, I blinked at what I was sure must be an apparition. Not thirty feet away, coming up the sidewalk . . . Albert!

This was absolutely insane. We had parted company three days earlier, almost two hundred miles away, neither of us at that time having any thought of coming to Krakow. Yet, here we were, synchronistically converging at the same point in time and space.

Albert was as stunned as I — the only time I ever saw him lose his cool. Gorza understood nothing of our wide-eyed encounter until I was coherent enough to tell her, and then she looked at me as if I had performed a miracle — as if I'd had anything to do with it! But it turned out so perfectly for me that I could understand her awe. Albert was heading for Prague the next morning, and so was I! I would already have had my rail ticket, but for being short on zlotys that morning, when I went for it.

Before dark that evening, in a final gesture of hospitality, Greg and Gorza took me to a hilltop overlook, somewhat west of town, to see the entire city bathed in sunset. A score of church spires spiked upward, glinting gold like a troop of spear-bearing angels; and the fortress rampart of Wawel Castle marking the southern reach of ancient Krakow was once more aglow in Medieval glory, as only the brief image called forth by a sunset can reveal. The Wisla River flowed around the rocky rise on which the castle stood — the same Wisla that courses through Warsaw and on to the Baltic Sea.

We talked with some young fellows who had also come for the view, one of whom bore such an uncanny resemblance to my brother when he was young – even in his laugh and way of speaking, though he spoke no English at all – that I had a sudden flash my visit to Krakow had been no accident at all, but the likely urge of my mongrel roots to find their home. It had taken an assortment of happenings to overcome my resistance to traveling Eastern Europe, to begin with, and then a further push by accidental events all along the way, to route me toward Krakow. The incredible encounter with Albert only served to confirm it — for that is the apparent point of synchronicities: to affirm hidden realities . . . to make them irrefutably obvious, unconditionally believable.

In Albert's immediate travel arrangements, my standing had slipped to that of 'fifth wheel' — or fourth wheel, anyhow. He had somehow latched onto two other travelers, both women, and I had to take a back seat. It was actually a blessing, for it somewhat shielded me from the worst effects of his driving. Poor Beverly was now in the hot seat, and more than once I could see her suddenly stiffen, or hear the slight catch in her voice as Albert continued to put his car through its paces. She was on her way home to San Francisco, flying from Prague. Our other companion, sharing the rear seat with me, was Stephanie, a young Canadian in temporary residence there. Albert, of course, was on his way back to Germany but wanted to cap his holiday with a couple days in Prague.

I had meant to spend a few days there, myself, but hadn't expected that I'd be putting five days into Poland. The scheduled date for Dresden was crowding me now; and I realized, further, that to remain in Prague over a weekend – for it was now Saturday – would simply crowd my visit into the worst two days for it. I decided, by the time we got there, just to stay the night, and make a point of returning later in my journey for a more substantial visit.

Albert was careful to stop for gas on the Polish side of the border, and for good reason. We had zlotys to dispose of and there was no better way. In fact, no other way at this point, for there was no place left to spend them. I was up to my neck in zlotys. After feeling so smug about averting the purchase of a rail ticket to Prague, I realized now that it saved me nothing at all, for I had already made the exchange – fifty deutschemarks – in anticipation of buying the ticket. I now had more than 300,000 zlotys with me and they were totally useless outside the country.

So I became a major financier for this journey to Prague, putting 210,000 zlotys into it, or $18.50, which was more than the rail fare would have been. I consoled myself that it was the decent thing to do, for Albert had chauffeured me most of the way from Germany. And after all, I so seldom get the opportunity to repay my hosts . . . but I'm not at all sure that Albert had any appreciation for the novelty of that event.

Episode 10.3

Tachycardia!

Klaus took me, that evening, on a native's guided tour through the historic heart of Nürnberg. Up alley passages, down stone stairways, between ancient walls and into charming courts — I only realized how well he knew the place when I tried to retrace some of our trail the following day, and couldn't do it, even with a map in my hands. One particularly fascinating item was a half-timbered two-story structure, its beams intricately 'keyed' to each other in such a way that they locked securely into place with no use of nails or pins! The building had been slated for demolition, he told me, until a last minute x-ray probe revealed the old structure beneath an outer facing that had covered its ingenious craftsmanship for as long as local tradition or record could recall.

We ended up in the northwest corner of the old section at the Tiergarten Platz, an open area of intimate size in the shadow of a great gate tower that pierces the old city wall here. A quiet gathering spot for evening crowds who sit and stand around as if something were about to happen — but they, themselves, are the happening. As the soft amber lighting of outdoor beer and 'eis' gardens (ice cream) took over from the deepening twilight, it was a lovely scene: people in chatting/laughing/singing clusters, a pair of young women doing a juggling routine, an organ grinder and his monkey . . . and back-dropping all of it, lit by yellow floodlight, the looming Imperial Castle and its grandiose stable house – now Bavaria's most popular youth hostel – its high sloped roof raked by successive tiers of dormer windows thirstily open to the evening breeze. Altogether, a summer's evening ambience that was hard to leave, even though I was exhausted from the long day.

The rest of that weekend provided the respite from travel and summer intensity that I sorely needed.

Over a sendoff breakfast on Monday morning, Klaus told me of the *Wanderjahre* tradition: the wandering year of a young apprentice who has learned his art and goes out to share his skills among the people he meets along the way, for sustenance and shelter. He can go anywhere during his wander, but cannot return home until the year is done. I thought about the circumstance that my own year abroad would reach fullness in just a little more than a month. But what had been my apprenticeship . . . the rarified art of living in innocence? Had I really become a journeyman at it?

Klaus cleared the dishes away and then took me in his zippy yellow roadster for what seemed a long ride out the highway toward Munich, finally arriving at a busy service stop on the autobahn, the perfect place from which to resume my Wanderjahre.

It was an unusually bright morning and I felt singularly alive and high as I walked to the far end of the service area, picked my spot and unhitched the pack on my back to set myself for another go at the road — when a sudden momentary catch between my chest and throat alerted me to something all too familiar; but I was too busy untangling myself from the pack to make the instant response it called for.

For those few seconds of delay . . . I blew it. A tachycardia attack had taken hold. My heart was speeding off like Klaus' yellow roadster, in a race with itself, and I had lost the moment to apply the brakes.

I can't recall how long I've been dealing with tachycardia. I do remember some scary times it has put me through, going back at least twenty years. It takes over the body with a sudden flush and weakness, and one can barely keep going at minimal energy level. It might take a half-hour or the whole day to run its course — I've never had the fear-free patience to wait and see. I work at stopping it, for there is no other choice. It takes the spine out of one's being, and the mind can be turned to nothing else while it's happening.

Over the years, I've learned a few methods for snapping the heartbeat back to normal, but like a bacterium that develops a drug-resistant strain each has run its course of effectiveness and no longer works for me. The only consistently reliable counter-measure has been a response in the first few moments of fluttering pulse: to stop everything and breathe deliberately and deeply, holding the first lung-full of air for a moment and then slowly and evenly letting it out all the way, doing a mental count at the proper rhythm. But the deep and slow breathing must begin immediately — before the tachycardia gains a momentum that is far more difficult to break.

The moment I realized it had gotten away from me I knew I was in trouble. With traffic pounding all around me, people looking at me from every direction (the idiotic things we worry about!), nowhere to hide, no place to go for help — as if I even knew what help to seek, miles out on the autobahn from Nürnberg . . . What to do?!

In dizziness and uncertainty, free of panic only because I hadn't the energy for it, I sat down cross-legged beside the onrushing traffic, put my earplugs into place and tried to find the calm for a return to deep breathing. But it was impossible, trapped between that maelstrom out there and the one going on inside my head.

I looked desperately around for a way out of the maddening highway situation. A restaurant stood nearby, but the last thing I wanted was a social setting that required any effort at normalcy. I wanted to be alone somewhere. I saw a path to the side of the restaurant going through the trees, and I followed it — into a sheltered, rustic garden area curiously graced with a small stone Celtic cross, and no one in sight. A narrow bench faced the cross, a seating for one, as if it had been ordered for the very moment. I sat down to figure out what next in this situation of no options.

I tried again to meditate there, but it just wasn't happening. I tried one of the tricks I learned years ago when an attack had once driven me to a Berkeley emergency ward: holding a deep breath as tightly as possible while trying at the same time, with all available force, to exhale it. It had worked for me then and maybe once or twice since. But it only resulted now in profuse sweating.

I considered getting someone to call for medical assistance . . . but that brought a whole other range of problems into prospect. No insurance, for one thing, and I was not quite ready to trade off my shallow funds for the riddance of my shallow heartbeat. Every avenue seemed hopeless. Must I get out on the road in this condition and try for a ride? How would I even handle it if I got one?

I'd once read a believable interview with a woman who led a hitch-hiking life, who said she'd continue to thumb when she became ill, and a doctor would pick her up. It sounds far-fetched, I know, but one rule of innocence is that the answer to any serious problem is to be found somewhere in one's immediate world. And it had always worked that way for me. I could hardly fault it even now, for this secluded glen at least gave me a measure of peace — however small the consolation. But what else was here for me?

After maybe an hour of this debilitated agonizing – which might have been a form of prayer, sitting there in front of a mystic cross, though I had no such conscious intent – a strange idea popped into my head. I recalled how medical attendants, in the case of a suddenly failed heart, would beat on a victim's chest . . . massively, with solid blows. Ready to try anything, I fisted my right hand and hit my chest over the heart as solidly as I could.

Nothing changed.

But I had pulled my punch, I thought. It's not easy to pound yourself that way with full abandon. I closed my eyes, tried to release myself to a total effort and did it again. Still nothing.

Once more, and a roundhouse swing, doing my damnedest this time to forget it was my own body I was slamming . . .

I rammed myself so hard that for a dazed moment I thought something was different . . . but it WAS different — I was breathing easily. I quickly grabbed a wrist to check my pulse and felt it steady and strong. The tachycardia was gone!

I sat there in an indescribable moment of relief, hardly daring to move lest it undo the results of that marvelous inspiration. I shall probably never know where it came from, whether out of left brain or right. Nor how I knew enough to keep trying until that successful third slam.

Back on the highway again, my spirits soared as only on a spring day. It felt like I'd been let free after standing on a gallows, or magically become a stripling despite my sixty-four years. It put me into a carefree, singing space, and when another hitch-hiker turned up not more than a few minutes later, a tall and gangly young fellow dressed in short pants and tank top with a big floppy-brim hat, I was quickly into conversation with him. From Hamburg, way to the north, and heading for Innsbruck, Austria, he spoke English easily and was a good deal curious as to how I found the hitching "at my age." (Ha! . . . If he but knew.) The implication, of course, was that drivers would hardly be stopping for an old man. And even as I pointed out, in reply, that all kinds of people sit behind the wheel, one actually – then and there – pulled over for me.

For the two of us, as it turned out. A middle-aged fellow going to Munich, and he spoke only German; but the gods, now working smoothly for me, had provided a translator in my sudden roadside friend. I saw to it that he took the front seat, while I sat in the rear. It wasn't long before we stopped so they could switch places up front — our driver apparently weary at the wheel from a long morning on the road. I silently gave it my blessing (for wasn't I now precisely at the center of Grace?).

Munich was hardly more than an hour away; and once there, we pulled into a parking area by a satellite rail station on the east side. I helped my Innsbruck-bound companion find his routing, through the transit maze on the station's wall map — I was getting good enough at this game to give assistance to a native! For me, the next stop would have to be a bank, via the subway downstairs. In good banana-peel form, I had once more let my pocket cash drop below the ten-dollar level.

I came out of the underground station literally 'agasp' at the sudden surround of ornate and colorful old architecture. I was in the Marienplatz, the heart of Munich's downtown, with the Rathaus – the city hall – towering in front of me; yet the entire mid-day scene of lunchtime shoppers and browsers was as peaceful as if their world stood still. An incredible contrast with Berlin's hectic midtown pace.

In the span of an hour I found the only bank in town providing VISA cash, and then the American Express agency where a small bundle of letters awaited. Not among them, however – and it gave me a momentary jolt – the expected packet from London that should bring my last batch of maps and Servas host lists for the countries I had yet to travel through.

Well, I'd be here until week's end, and it would surely arrive by then — my irrepressible optimism falsely assured me.

Up alongside the Great Spine ... at 71

I returned to Europe for a brief visit in '97, with only a bit of hitch-hiking but enough to whet my appetite for it again. Having no good excuse for a hitching jaunt, I just decided to visit a few friends along the eastern flank of the Rockies. I did it in the late spring of the following year, after turning 71. Many warned me that hitch-hiking is no longer a trifling matter on the American scene, but it was fully as good for me as ever — a lovely reprise of outrageous displays of the providence that typifies my own open road.

I just might be the only hitch-hiker who has ever flown somewhere for no better reason than to thumb his way homeward. I didn't want to waste my energy on the long trip south from Seattle, so I flew into Phoenix and bussed from the airport there to Tucson so as to avoid the confusions of a major city.

I was remembering a smaller Tucson, of course, but it is still not so hard to hitch out of. A local bus put me right out at the Interstate, where I got my first ride in an open pickup — a superb way to begin such an adventure, for the sheer defiant quality of the experience . . . the slipstream of wind threatening to dislodge me at every bump in the road as we sped by signboards with that ubiquitous slogan of modern-day, risk-free America: "Buckle-up, Arizona, it's the Law!"

I rode about forty miles that way to the little town of Benson, from where I called my too-long-out-of-touch friend, Erika, who drove fifteen miles to pick me up. She'd have come for me in Tucson but after six years off the road I needed that ice-breaker, before I could feel comfortable with what I was up to.

Then it was four days of laid-back relaxation, divided between Erika and Ken who live apart from one another and split the parenting of little Casey — whom I was meeting for the first time. Unwittingly, I had begun my journey just before a holiday weekend and preferred to wait it out before going back on the road. Among other diversions, we spent an afternoon in Tombstone and just happened to turn up on their annual Wyatt Earp Days observance. Every sort of Old West sartorial finery was on hand, his and hers; and there must have been fifty versions of Doc Holliday around town, I swear, each looking fancier and more dangerous than the last. It was fun.

Early Tuesday morning, I was back out on the road at a freeway access outside the little town of Willcox. Before the day's heat got underway, but not too early for the headtrips that plague a hitcher at a lonely outpost — especially one who has no idea, yet, what to expect of this highway, and these times. Sure, I'd gotten a ride out of Tucson, but Willcox is a much more remote spot; and the pickup ride, for that matter, could easily have been a fluke. These are the kinds of thoughts that stake out a territory as one dips into the hitch-hiking stream.

It only got worse after an hour had passed… and worse yet after two, before that ultimate calm point arrived at which the two parts of the horizon merge, and the road – with its trickling pace of traffic – simply turns into the path of life, no longer obstructed with judgements and what-ifs. *Que sera, sera.* And then, a half-hour beyond, a big white truck and trailer rig paused for me after turning onto the ramp slope.

This is one of the best hitches to be had — roomy and comfortable, always a long ride, and infused with an indescribable feeling of quiet power, which is surely the apotheosis of that carnal contraption called the automobile. There is a certain regal quality to riding in a big rig as a passenger.

They are likely breaking rules by picking anyone up. My host, in this instance, was an Hispanic, a people whose charitable instincts are closer to the surface, as I've many times found, than in most of us gringos.

He was headed for El Paso, so I had a ride all the way to Las Cruces — 200 miles. But I may have made a tactical error in going that far, ignoring Ken's advice to take the shortcut at Deming. One thing about hitch-hiking, all too easy to overlook, is that it puts one into a different reality stream, in which randomness no longer applies and everything has to be considered for its possible meaning. Advice is not idle conversation, but often a meaningful message from the gods, or however you wish to define its source.

At any rate, I did not get another ride that day. I spent most of the afternoon finding my way around Las Cruces, a much more sprawling place than I recall from twenty years ago, the situation hardly helped by my unaccountable and greenhorn failure to do the prime first thing in such circumstances: get a map of the territory! I can only attribute this lapse to what happens when an aging fool fails to stay in touch with the faculties and skills of earlier years. "Use it or lose it," as they say. Local maps are ridiculously easy to obtain these days in any phone booth with a directory, and it will normally provide transit information as well.

The problem in Las Cruces, however, was more complex than a map could easily have resolved. I never did find a primary or best freeway entry. I spent two late-afternoon hours at one that provided almost no shoulder space for cars to pull over, before fortune favored me with another hitch-hiker walking in off the Interstate. I thought at first it was a burly, baggage-laden fellow, but it turned out to be a woman — one of those rare 'Ladies of the Road,' tanned by it and obviously an old hand at this way of travel.

She nodded at me in an easy way, and I asked if she knew of any better on-ramp than this one. She came back with the advice that I should just get out on the Interstate, itself. I had worried the hazard of being stopped by police, and she assured me that they ignore freeway hitch-hikers in New Mexico, despite the fact that the posted signs prohibit it.

"I do it all the time," she said. "They won't bother ya." And then she was gone, before I could even work up to a decent conversation and maybe get a little of her story, which must certainly have been interesting.

I took a break, then, for a bite to eat, and went out on the highway for the remaining hour of daylight. But all the value I got out of it was another hitcher walking up the freeway who paused for a brief exchange, telling me where I could find a 'mission' in Las Cruces if I needed a night's free lodging.

It is really amazing, how the road-reality works to take care of me, whatever the situation — and I have never seen it fail! But this night was warm enough – and I was in sight of what seemed a good, removed spot to lay out my sleeping bag – that I opted against doing the long walk in search of the mission shelter. I bedded down under a desert willow in fragrant bloom and was rewarded at dusk with a whole swarm of hock moths coming for their evening meal. If you've never seen these fanciful little creatures, they are like miniature hummingbirds, doing exactly the same thing as hummingbirds — nosing into the honey-pods with a siphoning beak that is almost as long as their inch-plus bodies. They neither bothered me nor bothered with me, but went about their own nourishment, though only inches away from where I lay. A pure twilight treat.

The night was not, however, as restful as I'd have liked, because of all-night high intensity lighting not far enough away from me. And worse, I awakened at 2 a.m. to the realization that I was not handling a hard-ground bed as well as I used to — another instance of the 'use it or lose it' imperative. I had suddenly become a very old man with aching joints, and worse yet, terrible cramping in my legs when I tried to turn over. But I got back to sleep, and was up at the count of six (hours), ready for another crack at getting out of Las Cruces.

This time, ready for full freeway exposure and having the necessary map and transit info, I made my way to the very last access ramp out of town, which required almost a mile of walking beyond the bus stop closest to it. I should note that I was carrying only 20 pounds of baggage, but there were times when it felt like forty.

Once again I found myself in a two-hour holding pattern, with the creeping suspicion that anything I might have gained from exposure to the full freeway traffic flow was probably cancelled by the loss of what a first rate access road so beautifully provides: a moment of slowdown, and eye-to-eye contact with drivers in a position to be responsive. But it is ever the nature of hitch-hiking to entertain these misgivings, which have little or nothing to do with that flash of a moment when the ride – the right ride, the only possible ride – comes along.

My driver this time was a young fellow about 40, on his return commute from the State College in Las Cruces to Truth-or-Consequences, about 75 miles up the road. (Yes, there really is a town named Truth-or-Consequences — or, as the natives say, 'T-or-C'). We launched into immediate conversation. His name was Mark, a fellow who seemed in almost desperate need of someone he could really relate to. He was basically a rover, trying to settle down in a narrow-consciousness part of the country where few could identify with him. Circumstances had led him here, but it was more a case of bearing with it than really getting into it. I took his address, because I wanted to send him some material that might help. Which was a very good thing, because . . .

He drove me to the end-of-town freeway ramp in T-or-C, and 45 minutes later I had my next ride, a fellow of such high-riding consciousness that I knew almost at once it was the perfect connection for Mark. Not only did both of them live in T-or-C, but Jack (this next driver) was actively engaged in supportive work with people, in various contexts. He called himself a 'light worker,' in the metaphysical sense, and had no hesitation picking up on my suggested contact with Mark.

The hitch-hiking had suddenly seemed to fall into place, as though I had found the old groove, and I was feeling the exhilaration that comes with synchronicities like this — the sense of being in touch with a deeper flow of meaning and actually an integral part of the lives I interact with on the road. This is hitch-hiking at its very best, and most exquisitely so when one is conscious of it while it's happening. But the biggest 'hit' with Jack had not yet come.

He drove me directly to the address of my next destination in Albuquerque – 150 miles onward from T-or-C – and when we got there he did a kind of slow draw double-take . . . "What did you say their name was?"

When I repeated it for him, he told me he knew them. Which hardly says it — he was the one, I eventually discovered, who first introduced this couple, John and Patricia, to each other! And they know him as someone who seems always to turn up on some kind of unusual cue.

Jack had told me that he picked me up on the road, back there, because of some recalled friend who'd spoken of having had to hitch-hike when a truck broke down and having seen some roadside graffiti that said, "been here three and a half days waiting for a ride" — all of which may have been true, but I suspect our interaction had more profound roots, from all of what ensued. He was even familiar with Vocations for Social Change, the young Canyon Collective that long ago gave me the start with *Black Bart*. Jack was like a voice out of the past, suddenly there in the New Mexico desert lifting the level of everything that took place.

I knew Patricia mainly from the Internet, as a participant in an online synchronicity list, which further heightened the impact of all that had just happened. Her place was spacious, and wonderfully recuperative as I stayed through that night and the next. And then, on Friday morning, I was handed a 400-mile ride to Denver, a gift of the gods, in the persona of a nephew of John's who just happened to be going my way at the perfect moment. Do you doubt, at all, that I was now 'in the flow' of things?

James (the nephew) drove me right to the doorstep of my next host, Rosie, a *Black Bart* reader of many years' standing, who hosted me for two nights of good, stimulating conversation, after which I proceeded to Boulder by local bus, to touch bases with a few more *Black Bart* friends: Toni (for the third time we've seen each other in 25 years), and on the outskirts of town there was Arden, a hitch-hiker, himself, in college days and even recently. He put me up for that last Colorado night in Boulder, and memorialized the occasion for me with a photo of us both.

Now the trip begins to get spacy, for the Denver/Boulder area is like civilization's last outpost along Interstate-25. Forgive me, Cheyenne, but that's a hitch-hiker's take on it. The game tightens up, and I could only hope that I'd become ready for it.

The outermost local bus took me into Longmont, and a half-mile walk took me out to where the road becomes highway. Highway of an old-time sort, like they used to be in the 1940s when they simply eased out of town, with plenty of space for pulling over and no encouragement to floorboard the gas pedal. I was not long in snagging my ride, a six-miler out to I-25 with an ordinary guy who wanted to tell me about how he had recently been stunned when his wife ran off with a fellow ten years her junior. He was hurting, and I gave what support I could in a ten-minute session.

He left me at a windy, dusty, 'detour' access where a lot of roadwork was being done — a decent flow of traffic, but not the setting to entice a pull-over. I waited almost an hour for a computer consultant (who didn't look like one), who took me 25 miles to the Ft. Collins exit. I got there just ten minutes before another hitch-hiker, a late-morning riser who sauntered up from a patch of shrubbery where he had spent the night. Demonstrating a well-honed grasp of the ways of the road, he was decent enough to settle down almost out of sight with a book, and leave me my territorial privilege.

Within a half-hour, my third ride in this series came along — a woman with her youngster in a pickup, in some vast hurry, the reason for which I never did understand, as the roaring wind and motor combination made it impossible to hear and pretty-well dampened any conversation for the fifteen miles that I rode with her.

The exit she dropped me at was just about in the middle of nowhere. But the bleakness had hardly begun to trouble me when it was displaced by the odd sight of a car backing all the way up the on-ramp. It puzzled me for only a moment before I realized he was doing it for me. It's not unusual to get one of these 'second thought' lifts, but having it happen like this, as if I were a magnet pulling him back to me, can be considered a rare form of entertainment . . . as well as hospitality.

This guy was a real gem. He not only took me the remaining forty miles to Cheyenne, but he drove me out to the fringe of town for a particular mail-order clothing house I wanted to check out (after advising me that it was impossible to get there by public transit), waited for me while I bought several pair of hard-to-find liner socks that I could not have ordered without eyeballing them, took me all the way back to the other edge of town (at the highway we'd come in on) where he tried unsuccessfully to flag another ride for me with his CB radio, and then took me back into town to let me off at the address of a hostel that I had prior information about.

I didn't have the nerve, sadly, to have him wait while I checked it out, for it turned out to be a dud. It was listed on the Web as a $14 hostel, but it was only a seedy hotel with rooms at $16 plus tax. Granted, there wasn't much difference, but just enough to raise my hackles — that, and the incredible attitude of the woman at the desk, who was offended to the point of outrage that I should even broach the matter of what was on the Web. So I walked.

Out the door, I wasn't quite sure of what next. The possibility of a dorm bed for the night had softened my willingness to go immediately onward; besides which, those were Wyoming-size distances that my recent gem of a driver had been showing me, out to the Interstate from the center of town.

I wandered up the street with no particular direction in mind, passed a radio station and thought it might be a good place to look for transit info. No one at the desk, so I busied myself with the phonebook on it until a young fellow emerged who seemed a catalog of useful info about Cheyenne. Before I knew it, we were off to a late lunch together — I being at pains to reject his offer to pay for mine. After all, I have to maintain some level of dignity!

The upshot was that he gave me an orientation to this rather amazingly hospitable outpost, even the address of a possible shelter for strays like myself, nicely located on the road out of town. Covering all possible exigencies, I also learned there was only one bus a day from Cheyenne to Billings, my next intended destination, and it left at 12 noon. There was this nagging fear of getting utterly stranded in mid-Wyoming, nowhere near any place that a bus might stop — the sort of torment at which the left-brain absolutely excels.

By the time I finally walked out toward the Interstate, there was not much left of the day. The shelter proved a good lead and I might have taken it, but just before I got out there I happened across a wonderfully adequate outdoor spot — a clean and fairly roomy piece of level ground alongside a motel, but completely surrounded by shielding shrubbery.

What had been a balmy evening turned cold after dark. My lightweight bag wouldn't have made it, but I had long underwear with me and managed to hold my own. But for that mild edge of discomfort and a few mosquitoes before I got my netting up, I got a decent night's sleep, my body having toughened considerably since that occasion in Las Cruces.

Morningtime, and I was out on the road again by 9 a.m. – right out on the Interstate this time – after a pancake breakfast, aware that in two hours I'd have to deal with that question about the day's Greyhound. My resolve, at this point, was to accept only the long ride, and I hoped my sign, "Billings" (Montana), had big enough lettering for an onrushing freeway driver to see. Anything less than all the way would risk a stranding.

Now, the worst thing one can do, on the open road, is to challenge the Universe — which is done with signs and time-limits. I knew this, but . . . That old left brain is a mischievous and demanding devil.

Two hours went by and I was on the very edge of throwing in the towel, when along came a rather battered old car driven by a cheerful, down-home sort of guy with a receding chin and a moustache that made him look like Ben Turpin (known only to old movie buffs). He had been driving all night from Nevada, on his way to visit a girlfriend in Dakota, had just let off an earlier hitcher before he spotted me, and told me flat out that he'd be heading off east in another 70 miles, after Wheatland.

Well, my basic inclination to ride with whatever comes took over, and I just got in. So much for signs and resolves. When we reached his exit there were a few service facilities on hand, but little else could be said for it. The Interstate traffic, by this distance, was down to a trickle and my spirits dropped to about that level, too. The little nag inside of me was saying that I'd blown it for sure.

Amazingly, however, I had my next ride in half an hour, as unlikely a ride as I could have imagined. A spiffed-up rancher with a Western drawl and a ten-gallon hat, and a pair of prize horses in trailer-tow, was heading 80 miles up the line to Glenrock. And he filled me with all the lore about Wyoming I'll ever want to know — the wheat economy, the marble industry (counter-tops from silicon-bonded marble dust!), the great coal fiasco . . . if it happened in Wyoming, I got an earful of it; even a belabored history of Chugwater, with which I have a family connection of sorts. All the while, I was gloating that I'd gotten onward from Wheatland, and never mind that the ride would fall twenty miles short of Casper, the only sizable town in mid-state Wyoming.

But I didn't yet know that Glenrock was a couple miles off the highway, and that the junction he'd leave me at had absolutely nothing that would facilitate any slowdown of traffic or pacify my anxieties thereat. Not a thing — zilch, null, zero, nada, it was as barren as Patrick Stewart's shiny pate! I was too dazed at the sight of this deadfall I had let myself into to even notice, as I shouldered my pack to cross the road, exactly where the next mirage appeared from; but very suddenly in front of me was a clunker of a car with a rather wild-eyed young woman leaning out, asking if I needed a ride into Casper!

As I've said before, sometimes I can't even believe my own reality. I was inside the car before she could change her mind, doing my best to explain to the couple in the front seat – a kind of modern-day, generation-x version of Bonnie & Clyde, judging from the attire and their world-be-damned attitude – that I hadn't had a vehicle breakdown somewhere, but was actually hitch-hiking, yes, at 71! The guy was totally amazed; he'd thought I was about 50. You have to give these kids credit for seeing below the surface of things.

Actually, they landed me two miles short of Casper at a place called Evanston. They figured it was the best place for me to hitch onward from, a first-rate truck stop. I took time out for a late lunch, there, and discovered there were telephones at each table, so I used my Working Assets card to make a couple calls — one home to Joy, and another to Greyhound, to check on the local status. The Billings bus – the one out of Cheyenne – ran from Casper at 4:30 — I was still an hour and a half ahead of it! But I got another piece of vital information: for only twice the fare to Billings, I could have my passage all the way home, with as many stopovers along the way as I cared to take.

What really made up my mind, however, was a weather report on the radio channel entertaining the diners. A cold spell was heading into the area with a 40% chance of precipitation, which might even include a touch of snow. So I was once again caught between the bus option and the sketchy possibilities of open-road Wyoming, with the ante getting steeper than I wanted to bet.

By the time I made up my mind, after a useless twenty minutes on the road, it was 3:30. The bus terminal was at least two miles away, and I was not willing to pay the $7–8.00 taxi fare quoted to me over the phone, so I set out on a forced march along the freeway. I made it with fifteen minutes to spare, got my Seattle ticket for $98, and it was all over except for the applause.

Well, not quite. There was a hitch-hiking coda up the line.

I spent two recuperative days in Roundup, MT with friends Wilbur and Elizabeth, whom I hadn't seen in some twenty years, and who – along with their college-age daughter, Rhiannon – met me that night in Billings. It did get down to 38° and we hit rain squalls before getting there, vindicating the decision

— though I'm sure the road gods would have somehow seen me safe had I chosen to do otherwise.

There was one more couple I wanted to see in Montana, at Kalispell, which called for a 115-mile sidetrip at Missoula from the bus ride homeward. That's where I hitched again, rather than pay the $16.75 fares each way, and it was a great little finale to the larger journey, almost a reprise of it — a tale worth telling in its own right.

Two rides getting up to Kalispell and one for the return. As earlier on the journey, I felt I was fulfilling a supportive role with the first of these drivers, making the continuance of a counter-cultural consciousness real for him and the sense of a grand – if often hidden – network of earth-concerned people a positive reality. We discussed the book, Ishmael, by Daniel Quinn, and some of the insights I had been given on the road.

He took me just fifteen miles, from which point another of those instant rides came along (like 'Bonnie and Clyde') — I was merely walking toward a good positioning spot when a Native American named Billy pulled up ahead to wait for me. I'd had my thumb out, but he only had a view of me from the back.

A lot of interesting conversation with Billy, but the main thing I'll remember was the bowl of chili. He stopped for gas and offered to buy me a meal if I was hungry, but I politely declined. Next thing I know, he is thrusting this giant cardboard bowl of chili at me in the car! Well, I am not a chili man. I hadn't had a taste of chili since 1948, and I'm sure I'd have turned down a bowl if it was the last morsel of food I'd see for a week (or the first after it) . . . I'm not into the meat, I'm not into the heat (spices) and I'm not into the beans. But this big Indian was not going to take no for an answer . . . pure, simple generosity, and I couldn't get out of it.

So I ate it. Every blessed spoonful of it. And before done with it, I was eating with gusto, for – I hate to admit this, but ... I found I liked it!

Lois and Matt are old California friends who moved here from Arcata a couple years ago, and I spent the full weekend with them, catching up, letting down, and generally enjoying myself. When the Monday morning time came to resume my journey home, I had every intention of doing it in a civilized fashion — on the bus. But I couldn't resist giving one final hour to the road, instead of sitting in a dowdy bus terminal — giving it a healthy try, at least, before buying my bus ticket. I was on the highway near the bus station at 9 a.m.

As earlier, I was dead set on a ride going all the way, if I were to take any at all, as the bus out of Missoula to Seattle would be leaving at 1:40 p.m. and there was little leeway for dalliance. I waved off one driver offering a ride to "the junction," wherever that was. But when this young fellow in a pickup pulled up, and said he was in a hurry, hop in, I just barely got the nod that he was going to Missoula and made my commitment.

As we got to talking, I discovered that he wasn't actually going to Missoula, but around it, heading on to Helena, where a grandfather was dying and he had to get there before it was too late. He had been too late for another grandfather, and an uncle, under similar circumstances, so his concern was justified. He paused to take me aboard only because he wanted the leveling influence of some company until he could pick up his Mom and Pop, a few miles this side of Missoula.

From his motorized standpoint, he was going to Missoula, but the highway actually bypasses the town, and it put me suddenly at risk again, of getting stranded. He simply didn't have the time to detour into town for me, but had it in mind to let me off at a juncture highway about five miles out. He figured

I could get another easy lift from that distance, but nothing is so nerve-jangling and feckless as trying to get a ride – of any distance – under critical time pressure.

So here it was: Cheyenne and Casper all over again. But I had a job to do on this ride, and kept him talking about his Grandpop, his family, and sundry other things. Along about the time we stopped for his folks – at which point I had to get in the back of the pickup – we re-strategized and he agreed to put me off at a closer-to-town exit, just two miles from the bus depot. From there, I could walk it.

So I ended my hitching just as I had started it: in the back of a pickup truck, and something short of where I was headed. I got to the station just as the bus from Kalispell was pulling in, and twenty minutes before its Seattle departure time.

I'm not overly fond of these photo-finishes, but they do make the journey more memorable. And somehow, they always seem to happen.

Echoes in the Twilight (2000-03)

That wonderful 1998 adventure was something of a 'last hurrah' for my hitch-hiking days, and I was well aware of it at the time. But the urge to hit the road doesn't just quietly go away, when there are so many lovely memories of more vigorous times. It is reborn with the seasons, and not even the winter of life can entirely dampen its annual emergence.

The story of how Robin Hood weakly sent his last arrow flying through an open castle portal to land where they should lay his weary body to rest has always fascinated me, and I've sometimes wondered if my ultimate fate is to wander off on a truly final road trip, waving my thumb to the very last.

But that, if so, is still a ways off — and meanwhile, there is always the seasonal return. I've given in to it twice, so far, and these are the tales of those late-life echoes of the beat. The first was very brief, just a few hours of mid-Oregon thumbing to get me from Eugene to one more Earthstewards Gathering that took place just beyond the range of public transportation. I might have arranged for a ride with someone, but I thought I'd try doing it, one more time, my own way. The second had an entirely different rationale and nobody could have talked me out of it, even with an offered ride as an alternative actually at hand. You'll see why when you get into it.

Each instance, however, took its toll on my diminishing energy and roadside staying-power; each was clearly telling me, "Hey, old man, it's time to pull in your thumb and call it quits!" By any common-sense reckoning, it certainly is.

But 'common sense' does not reckon with the impulsive spark of spring or the rolling thrust of summer, and I cannot assure that I won't respond again. I do regard these closing tales as the closure of my footloose trail . . . but don't be at all surprised if you should happen to see someone who looks like me out there, again at the side of the road, thumbing for your charity.

If we should meet that way, you'll likely be part of the magic that never fails to attend my road trips. As you'll plainly see, from these last two tales.

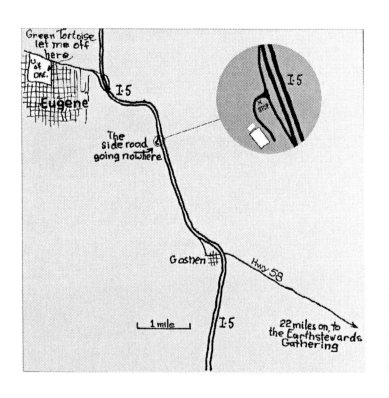

Episode 12.1

Three Mistakes

I guess my first mistake was the assumption – without even
checking it out – that the Green Tortoise bus would cheerfully
pull off the highway for a moment where I wanted to get off. I
was remembering the Green Tortoise of an earlier era, when
that was a 'no problem' request. Today, it requires an additional
$10 for the service — and my indignation is grounded in my
habituated penury. Ten dollars for a 4-mile distance beyond
Eugene? No way!

But call it something closer to penny-wise and pound-foolish,
for it subjected me to more roadside aggravation than the $10
saved was probably worth.

My project was to hitch-hike from I-5, along the secondary
Highway 58 near Eugene, OR — the final 18 miles to a
country side-road, down which the annual Earthstewards
Gathering was happening. The Green Tortoise would arrive at,
and depart Eugene at 3:00 p.m. on Thursday afternoon, and
the proceedings of the Gathering were to begin at 6:00 p.m.
with an Opening Circle, and then dinner. The time-gap was

loose and easy — a 'snap' for a hitch-hiker, even in unfamiliar territory. Central Oregon is populated with good people.

The Green Tortoise driver made it easier to make the choice I did – to leave the bus at Eugene – by telling me that a local bus actually ran out Highway 58 for the full distance I had to go. So my second mistake was taking his word for it.

Oh, he was telling the truth — it's just that the local bus only runs every four hours, and another wasn't due to leave Eugene until 5:30 p.m., which would leave me virtually no time at all for the final few miles that I'd still have to hitch. My third mistake was not waiting and taking that bus.

What eventuated, because of those three mistakes, was surely one of the most hassled 27 miles of time-driven hitch-hiking that I've ever put myself through.

It seemed to start well — with a quick ride scored for the mile-long distance to the I-5 on-ramp, from close to the University of Oregon campus where the Green Tortoise makes its local stop. But it was a poorly constructed ramp for hitching, and a half-hour there produced nothing at all for me. The realization, at this point, that any ride I might get could take me only four miles along I-5, anyhow – to Hwy. 58 – tended to magnify the time I was 'wasting' at this difficult spot.

At 4 p.m., and with time now ticking away in my head – the hitch-hiker's worst dilemma – I reviewed my options: 1) walk back into town to wait for the 5:30 local bus; 2) continue thumbing right where I was, taking the chance that I could lose option #1 by my delay; 3) take advantage of Oregon's 'walkable freeway' laws and head for a possibly better ramp situation, and the full freeway exposure as I went. At worst, with this last option, I'd walk the four miles to Hwy 58, and at a good clip I should make that in little more than an hour — so I chose option #3, and shouldered my pack.

Maybe I should call that a fourth mistake, for I was hardly capable, any longer, of taking on a freeway gradient in the hot Oregon sun with a 20-lb pack on my back, and doing it at any better clip than about two miles per hour. By the time I saw the mileage sign that told me the junction was still three miles away, it had begun to feel exhaustingly grim.

That's when an exit road appeared, as if conjured by magic, leading to a Texaco station and a coffee shop. Small succor, but maybe it held something for me. At least a break from this increasingly shadowed endeavor.

As I got closer, I could see it was indeed a cul-de-sac exit, just to those services. Anyone taking it had to return to I-5 by doing a jack-knife switchback to this same little side road I was approaching on, with – glory be! – an arterial stop at the point of the angled turn. One car made the stop just as I came up to it, with its window open . . . and nothing felt more natural than smiling into it and asking for a lift!

He couldn't help me, it turned out, because he was only going another mile down the freeway. But immediately behind him, a big SUV-style pickup made the same full stop — *for me*, it seemed, and I put the plea out to him. He was only going to Goshen, he said, and I told him that was exactly where I wanted to go. Still reluctant, but obviously trapped, he hesitated.

"Oh, all right, hop in the back" . . . as if his wide and otherwise empty cab seat just wasn't there.

I told him my 'hopping' days were behind me, "but just give me a bit of time and I'll do it." It took two tries before I lofted the old bod into the truck bed, and we were off and away.

One more time, at 73! — the wild pleasure of a windblown ride in an open, bouncing truck!

We reached Goshen in short order, and my reluctant host, having had a few miles to think about it, actually came around and lowered the tailgate for me so I could leave his truck with a bit more dignity than I got on board with. I am only here to help others realize their humanity.

Highway 58, however, was not the instant salvation I had anticipated. It took 45 minutes – to 5:30 (the Eugene bus departure time) – before a hippie couple in a VW came along and took me out to the branching country road. I was ahead of the bus that would have gotten me there, but it was now only 15 minutes shy of 6:00 p.m., and I still had 4.8 miles to go.

I unfolded the Earthstewards sign I had prepared in advance — though it was useless unless someone going by recognized what it was all about. But magically it happened that way, and within ten minutes! I actually got to the Gathering as the Opening Circle was getting underway.

I can't tell you, for sure, why hitching works that way for me, but it supports my conviction that reality is not merely its surface appearance. I think that as we live our lives we are also creating an energy web, to the same specs we live by, very much like a spider builds its own web, infinitely delicate and practically invisible, but supportive of the spider's way of life.

Episode 12.2

Just One More for the Road

Age 76 is nothing to joke about. Of course, I said that at 63, too, and had some very satisfying hitch-hikes yet to come. But I could tell from my brief road trip two years back that the body does, finally reach its limits of flexibility. The simple act of getting into or out of a car – let alone trying to clamber into the back of a pickup – becomes a sequence of creaking contortions. Nature will have her way, despite our protestations of it being all in the mind.

But events conspired, almost in spite of my *contrary* protestations, to urge me toward one more go at it. In the wintery season most recently past, a small assemblage of world-noteworthy hitch-hikers had taken place right here in Seattle. *Very* small, it consisted of only three hitch-hikers: Bernd Wechner, founder and longtime mediator of the world's most extensive hitch-hiking web network and bulletin board at Salon101.com (inactive at the time of this writing), Morgan 'Sal'man Strub, developer of America's own prime hitch-hike-network web site, digihitch.com, and myself. Maybe needless to note, I was there mainly because it took place right here in Seattle.

In being there, however, I found in Morgan someone who resonates entirely with my own sense of what the road experience is all about, in terms of a mystical side of consciousness. It was like discovering a twin brother, though he was quite less than half my age.

When I then subsequently learned that Morgan had a secondary project getting underway, a noble and ambitious vision to turn the hitch-hiking community toward its most natural exemplary expression as a roving community of goodwill works and doings, mediated through a new web site that he was calling roadbard.net; and too, that another hitch-hiker gathering was planned for Portland, Oregon, to further that vision, the prospect of going down seemed too inviting to let it pass me by.

I had a second prompt, much more personal, that focused my yearning at a hitch-hiking level of participation: this year of 2003 was the 60th anniversary of my first time on the road — and wouldn't it be lovely to cap that record with one final go at it?

But I was wary of making any commitment that might run head-on into the Northwest's notoriously uncertain weather patterns, so I said nothing of it to anyone — except a casual hint to a Midwest niece who only wanted to make sure I'd be around for a visit: I said it depended on when she arrived, as I intended to spend a few days away in Portland. When she offered to drive me down, I had no choice left but to politely decline it, telling her I planned to hitch-hike.

The day arrived bright and clear and I was on my way, taking the easy approach of bussing the first 60 miles by a local transit string that cost me only $1.75, to avoid messing with the mid-city traffic uncertainties of Seattle and Tacoma. I took it as an entitlement of my years — though I don't think it spared me any traffic uncertainties at all, as it turned out. Even so, starting from Olympia added a nice touch to this 60th anniversary road trip, as it honored the well-recalled night of shelter found in an Olympia used-car lot on that very first hitch-hike, so long ago.

It was an appropriate stepping stone, for the entire short journey became a remembrance of times past, celebrating both the joys and uncertainties of this remarkable way of discovery.

On the downside, I had to settle for a three-hour roadside wait before I could get onward from Olympia, and it was only a lift of thirty miles, to the town of Chehalis. But I didn't even ride that far; I took my leave five miles short of it, in Centralia, when I saw the opportunity for another way to celebrate this anniversary journey.

Only months before this, I had finally tracked an old pal of mine, from those long ago 1940s, to this very locale. AMTRAK had taken me right down for a brief surprise visit, our first in more than 50 years; and I was now blessed with the perfect moment to solidify our renewed friendship.

Ray had never hitched with me, but he had become the sole remaining link in my life to those early years of it — the only one left who could see in me both the hitch-hiking kid and the hitch-hiking old man, and reflect them back to me as one and the same. What could possibly be more appropriate to this occasion?

His local friends Ross and Wanda took me in, that night, and carted me off to the freeway junction to resume the journey next morning, even preparing a packed lunch for my early departure.

In quick time, a 45-mile lift to the outskirts of Longview came along, with a great guy who regaled me with tales of his prowess as an eBay trader, leaving no question unanswered about how it's done.

And then, after a brief wait, the final ride of my hitch-hiking life: a quaint bit of mockery from the Universe, leaving me with a closure memory of just how absurd and unpredictable the world can be, on such a trail as the hitch-hiker plies

The car that pulled over for me just outside of Longview had two men in it, and the back was so full of junk that the driver had to get out and shift it all so I could squeeze in. Clearly, I could not refuse his generosity, even though I had a doubt or two about the men.

The driver was the only one who spoke to me. The other was very nervous, could not sit still, kept tapping his feet (to no music), rubbing his hair, twitching in various ways — but he wouldn't say a word to me, which naturally made me a bit uneasy. He looked rather demented, in fact. They were on their way to Powell's, in Portland, to sell several boxes of used books, and I said it was a good place for me to get off, too.

All of a sudden, about halfway along our course, the driver pulls off on a nowhere exit, nothing in sight, and mumbles something I couldn't quite make out. So I say to him, "What's up?"

And he replies, in his own garbled way, "Suddenly got sleepy. m-m-m I've gotta get some rest . . . m-m-m been up half the night getting all this stuff together."

Before I fully grasp what that means, he is changing seats with his front seat passenger. The demented one is going to drive!

I probably should have gotten out. Though it was such an unlikely place for another lift, I'm glad I didn't. To be honest, however, I was thinking too slow, and we were headed back on the freeway before I had fully digested the situation. So the driver-who-was-now-the-passenger quickly dozed off, and the passenger-who-was-now-the-driver was unsteadily weaving down the freeway, barely missing cars as well as he could. And I was sitting there gritting my teeth, with my pack pulled in front of me as the only safety barrier I had.

It didn't keep me from seeing the danger, however, when he failed to brake in time for traffic suddenly slowed ahead. I withheld my warning yell an extra half-second, afraid of shocking him into a bad move, and it proved just long enough for him to see the danger himself and slam the brakes — which awakened his dozing partner with a start.

"What happened? What happened!" he yelled. "Did you hit something?"

The guy was really jolted, and ordered his friend to pull over and park, so he could take the wheel again. I suffered the entire episode in silence, very thankful that our incompetent passenger was not going to take us through the confusion of bridges marking the final entry into Portland, and I left their hospitality as soon as I was able to, before we ever got to Powell's.

So I completed sixty years of hitching, still alive and reasonably sound of mind and body – appreciative of the reprieve that let it happen – and made my way to the place called *La Palabra Cafe*, where I'd find Morgan and Krista, and receive the plaudits due me for the hardy venture. This time, other hitch-hikers showed up, as well as a reporter or two, who noted my record for posterity. I may, in fact, have the record longevity of any hitch-hiker in America today. Maybe the record longevity *ever* — who knows?

Well, we can't all be Nobel or Pulitzer winners — some of us have to take the leftover laurels.

211

Afterlude

The First American Hitch-hiker . . .

Could it ever be possible, I wondered, to discover who was
America's first, ever, hitch-hiker? Somewhere there must be a
record — perhaps a letter, or better a journal with the limited,
scrawled details; or maybe even a newspaper account . . . buried
somewhere like the well-known needle in a haystack. It has to be
somewhere, if only in fragmentary form. Surely, the first one to
have the inspiration had to have left some record of it.

For it must have been an inspiration — to have thought to
'invade' the privacy of *just anyone's* private automobile journey.
That was truly a bold and inspired idea, in a land where privacy
is almost as sanctified as the castle that is one's home; even
vagabonding has its own kind of treasured independence and
privacy, shared only with the closest of companions.

When, how, and to whom, did this idea of sharing with total
strangers originate?

An offspring of the automobile age, hitch-hiking does
have antecedents in the simple and free joy of the long hike
— the 'tramp' as it used to be called, before that word took on
a derogatory coloration; and also in the more roustabout and
definitely *déclassé* style of no-cost travel known as riding the rails,
or freight hopping.

But hitch-hiking is different in several respects from that
somewhat disreputable ancestor. Not leastwise in terms of
its documented history, for there is a plentiful amount of
background material to be found on the hoboes, vagrants and
crop tramps that plied the rails — far more than has turned up
for hitch-hiking. But there are distinguishing characteristics too.

While they share the common root of a wanderlust that has ever fired the vagabond imagination, and even a similar rebellious attitude toward constrictive social mores, the classic freight-hopper was by nature a more guarded, anti-social sort, living a risky and ruggedly self-sufficient life, which is not at all the hitch-hiking style (though it's often portrayed that way by a media that thrives on sensationalism).

The hitch-hiker is an eminently social creature whose passion for the open road is as much grounded in the satisfactions of human interaction as in the mileage scored. The best hitch-hiking trails written are tales of people encountered, not merely territory traversed. And more: the hitch-hiker is usually an individual of creative impulse, oftimes a writer, a poet, an artist or a song-spinner — or at least, the yearning to become one. It is, in fact, the creative urge to use the open road as grist in a larger project – whether known yet at a conscious level or not – that finally becomes the irresistible pull.

Society, on its treadmill drive toward the supremacy of commerce over art, and 'respectable' conformity over personal expression, has offered few legitimate outlets for this 'seeking of grist' on the open road — other than tourism, a term and terrain uncongenial to the creatively adventurous, who seek the unplanned, the unconstrained, and the fully open . . . road. The very possession of one's own automobile, in this context, becomes a burden on the spirit, for even as it enables freedom, it is an isolative, alienating sort of freedom.

Oh, yes, there are also hitch-hikers of momentary necessity and of occasional flippant convenience, but these soon return to the crowd and do not concern me here. I am writing about the uncommon souls who stay with it from choice — these are the passionate hitch-hikers. These are the ones who understand the open road as a flow of exchange between givers — one who gives a ride, and the other who gives . . . what? Sometimes merely a stretch of company, but often more: a willing ear, an artful conversation, an interesting tale, a bit of inspiration, the sometimes rare blessing of appreciation that comes with an inspiriting reflection of true service having been rendered by an act of roadside generosity.

These are not to be lightly regarded; they mark a very real gap between isolation and community in our daily world. If only briefly, two people, heretofore and otherwise complete strangers, have bonded awhile, enriching their common humanity and reinforcing their shared awareness of it.

Which, of course, was not a regular aspect of riding the rails, to return to the comparison I started with. Compassion, sharing and community are the (mutual) rewards of hitch-hiking, but not of freight hopping.

There must certainly have been a first hitch-hiker who realized this, or discovered it, and how could he or she possibly be found? It's a question that has been nagging me for years. It had to have occurred sometime in the first, or more probably the second decade of the twentieth century, at a time when both of my parents were around — but I had never thought to question their recollection while they were still within memory's range of it.

Had I even done that much, I might know far more than I do, because one of them surely would have spoken of my aunt Edith who was, herself, one of the earliest of hitch-hikers! I didn't discover this until long after she had passed on in 1982, and a tattered old scrapbook of hers eventually turned up. When only twenty, she and a year-younger girlfriend took to the road together for a summer-long vagabond journey from California to New York and there were newspaper clips to prove it. That was in 1920 — three years before the first documented use of the term, hitch-hiking, in print. One article refers to them as "Hiking, motorcycling, automobiling, riding in any vehicle that came along – but mostly hiking…"

I briefly thought I had found what I sought when I discovered that the visionary poet, Vachel Lindsay, had hit the road, himself, in 1912, walking and taking what came his way along a midwest stretch of the corn and wheat belt. Letters to a family member back home left no doubt at all that he'd had rides from strangers all along the way. Here is the relevant passage from a missive dated June 23, 1912, found in an anthology put together by Dennis Camp, *The Prose of Vachel Lindsay*:

> "When the weather is good, touring automobiles whiz past. They have pennants showing they are from Kansas City, Emporia, New York or Chicago. They have camping canvas and bedding on the back seats of the car, or strapped in the rear. They are on camping tours to Colorado Springs and the like pleasure places. Some few avow they are going to the coast.
>
> "About five o'clock in the evening some man making a local trip is apt to come along alone. He it is that wants the other side of the machine weighed down. He it is that will offer me a ride and spin me along from five to twenty-five miles before supper. This delightful use that may be made of an automobile in rounding out a day's walk has had something to do with mending my prejudice against it, despite the grand airs of the tourists that whirl by at midday. I still maintain that the auto is a carnal institution, to be shunned by the truly spiritual, but there are times when I, for one, get tired of being spiritual."

I was truly elated, until I realized that his passage lacked one essential element of the hitch-hiking process. There is no indication, either in this letter or any of them I could find, that he ever intentionally set his sails for gaining a ride. They apparently were offered by passing drivers; but it never seems to have occurred to Lindsay to forthrightly take a hand in the process himself.

Waiting for the offer does nothing at all to challenge the status-quo of alienating privacy that the automobile engenders. And it does not change the invited rider's status from a passive recipient into a hitch-hiker.

It occurred to me, only days before this book was ready to go to press, to have one more go at the search. I went for the Readers Guide to Periodical Literature, a set of very fat books that provide indexed access to just about everything ever published in the magazine world. I had done this before, but without a clear term of reference (like hitch-hiking) it quickly becomes an exercise in futility, for there are hundreds of articles each year under one or another subhead of Automobile – to name one likely category – with hardly the time to track very many of them to their actual text pages.

But I went for it one more time, resolved to put an afternoon into the effort, roaming only among the title listings to see if any fair possibilities stood out among them. I used an assortment of key terms: begging, driving, caravaning, tramping, wayfaring, vagabonding… and such. Each fat volume covered just a few years so I had to spend several hours just surveying titles, and I came up with something more than a dozen possibilities, which then had to be tracked to their actual texts.

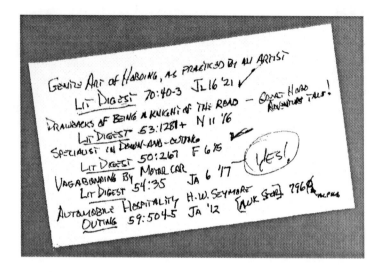

Amazingly, I hit the jackpot about midway through the list. There, in a *Literary Digest* article from the January 6, 1917 issue, buried in between word-packed ads for flower catalogs and bungalow plans, was precisely what I sought! More explicit, even, than I imagined it could have been.

The first American hitch-hiker turns up with the amusingly appropriate name, Charlie Brown (if I may take indulgent liberty with the more formal Charles that he, himself, used). He – as well as the reviewer who writes about him – conveys no awareness that anything at all like this has ever been done before, and takes us through the process of how it came to him. If the story can be relied on – and there is nothing on its face to indicate it can't – we have our man!

Here, then, is a full rendering of the revelational *Literary Digest* piece, making its debut re-appearance after 87 years hidden on library shelves . . .

VAGABONDING BY MOTOR-CAR

This is the tale of a man who rode more than a thousand miles in exchange for what totalled to twenty-eight "thank you's." That was his stock in trade, save for a clean collar, a genial smile, and an endless faith in human nature. And out of these he managed to make his way from Fort Wayne, Ind., to New York City, a distance of nearly a thousand miles, mostly over the famous Lincoln Highway.

The man is Charles Brown, Jr., a young Californian who is a student in New York University during the winter. But last summer, after an eventful vacation, he found himself stranded in Fort Wayne, with seven days until the opening of college, more than nine hundred miles away. All he had to do was to get the money for his railroad fare somehow, take a train, and come East. But all that was easier talked of than accomplished. In a recent issue of the New York World, Mr. Brown tells how it was done. He believes that faith in human nature can move mountains, and in his case, if it did not move mountains from his path, it at least moved him over them. He recounts to us:

It was in the freight-yards at Fort Wayne, Ind., on Wednesday morning, October 4, that I conceived the idea of traversing the Lincoln Highway in automobiles to New York City. I was stranded and almost without money, and for several days had been contemplating the chance of beating my way out on a freight.

As the railroad runs, New York City is nearly eight hundred miles distant from Fort Wayne. New York University, where I am an evening student, opening in seven days, and an editorial appointment to keep at the same time, it was a certainty that I must begin moving at once or fail to connect.

While I was sitting near a water-tank I saw an automobile speeding along the road that paralleled the tracks. It was a big touring car with a large and comfortable-looking seat in the rear. I could not take my eyes off the soft gray cushions. I watched the car pass out of sight; then my inspiration came.

As I left the freight-yards I counted my money. I had $4.50.

I went to a barber-shop and got a bath, then a shave and a hair-cut. I bought a clean shirt and a collar, also a clothes-brush and a can of shoe-polish. I had my hat cleaned and blocked and a new band put on. Then I found a tailor. While I sat with a blanket wrapt around me, he sponged and prest my clothes. I now had $1.55.

He was now ready to start for the metropolis, and accordingly he sought from the first policeman he met, directions about the best road going eastward. He was told to travel out East Main Street until he came to the Lincoln Highway.

He found that thoroughfare, and, noting the number of motor-cars passing, decided that it presented the most chances for a "lift" in the direction in which he was going. So he determined to stick to the road, hailing a car or two to help him on his way. He had very satisfactory luck, for he says:

About noon, after walking to the outskirts of Fort Wayne, I saw my first chance coming down the highway. At the steering-wheel of the car was a huge bulk of a man with tortoise-shell spectacles and coarse black whiskers.

Hardly knowing how I would stop him, I stept into the center of the highway. The next minute, afraid that he would ignore me, I stept back to let him pass, then suddenly ran forward and threw my hands up as a signal for him to stop.

"Are you going down the Lincoln Highway?"

"Yes, down a piece," he replied, stopping his car.

"May I ride with you until you turn off?"

"Where are you going?"

I moved close to the car, which was one of those democratic Fords.

"New York City."

His face registered interest, as he swung open the door nearest me. We struck out into the rural section. He was a physician, rushing to a girl patient whose condition had changed for the worse.

The interest increased as I explained my theory that a man, with courtesy and good clothes, could start at any point on the Lincoln Highway and get through to New York City within a comparatively short time by riding in different automobiles. People would enjoy giving him rides. As I was explaining the third time why a man need not carry any baggage on such a trip he slapped on the emergency-brake and told me to climb out, as his interest in my mode of traveling had caused him to run ten miles beyond his patient.

That night I slept in a barn. The next morning, after I had groomed two horses, a farm-hand brought me a plate of fried ham and potatoes. By six o'clock I was riding on a milk-truck. At nine o'clock an insurance agent invited me to ride with him until noon. In the afternoon I rode in a flivver with a school-teacher whose machine I had cranked. When it grew too dark I stopt at a farmhouse for the night and helped to husk corn.

Until I had ridden on the Lincoln Highway, I did not really know what beautiful country scenery was. Corn-fields yellowing in the early October sunshine stretched across Indiana, Ohio, and the western sections of Pennsylvania. Beyond came the Pennsylvania mountains, and then the Cumberland valley, rich in her robe of autumnal coloring. New Jersey was a series of panoramas, each more wonderful than the one preceding.

The longest single ride he had was 125 miles; the shortest less than 125 feet. The story of this latter ride furnishes a little comedy in itself, for we read:

It was at a time when I felt very much in need of a ride. The Pennsylvania mountains loomed ahead of me. I was afraid to cross them alone as a practical joker in Pittsburg had warned me that the mountains were swarming with moonshiners who might think me a Government inspector and "plug me full of lead" the first time I turned my back.

I had just put more shine on my shoes and brushed my clothes, when a machine stopt at the roadside. An old farmer and his wife asked me to ride with them.

"Be yer goin' to Bedford Springs, neighbor?" he inquired, as we got underway.

"No, New York City."

The old man started and turned half around with a look of suspicion: His fingers closed tightly on the steering-wheel. The machine swayed once or twice, then slowed down until it came to a stop.

The old man and his wife looked at me. The color had gone from their faces. It was evident that they thought me a doubtful character. The man fumbled at the door nearest me until it opened.

"No, we don't want to ride yer over them mountains. Yer might be" — "A highwayman?" I interrupted.

"I am — a Lincoln Highwayman."

During seven days I secured rides in twenty-eight automobiles, walking but a few miles. Some of the people who obligingly responded were: A baker who bought a new car when the price of bread was raised; a Pittsburg steel-manufacturer who will not fill orders for the Allies or for Germany; a music agent who, in order to demonstrate his goods, asked me to give an evening lecture on my travels at his place of business; a general merchant who let me sleep above his store; four ministers who make their parish calls in automobiles; several Ohio farmers; a county newspaper correspondent who intimated that if the price of print-paper continued to advance The Banner would have to suspend publication; three physicians; a farm demonstrator, and two jitney-drivers.

Democratic people, as a rule, drive inexpensive cars. Those who buy a new car each year invariably trade in their old one. I saw more flivvers and low-priced machines in Indiana and Ohio than in Pennsylvania and New Jersey.

In no instance was I refused a ride by a business or professional man. A physician straining all speed-laws to reach a dying patient or a banker burning up the road to make a directors' meeting by ten o'clock were not in such a hurry that they could not stop for me.

221

People riding for pleasure or on Sunday had no time or no room for me in their cars. I consoled myself with the reflection that in going after pleasure they lost it in that they missed the pleasure which comes from conversing with a Highwayman.

In Indiana and Ohio the people seemed glad to give away rides. In return I assisted in small ways: by watching the highway signs along the road, reading disfigured directions on sign-posts at cross-roads, running across a field to inquire of a farmer how to get back on the Highway after a detour, helping repair punctured tires, pouring oil and water into the machine, and tightening loose brakes.

Some day I am going to apply for a strip of the Lincoln Highway. I shall put in an elaborate system of toll-gates and appoint my friends as toll-collectors. Part of the money will be used for the up-keep of the strip, the remainder we shall keep for our own.

The above idea came to me while riding through Pennsylvania from Lancaster to Philadelphia. I gave up counting toll-gates long before the last one was reached. The tolls amounted to about $2 for a little less than seventy miles. A road association collects these tolls for the up-keep of the Lincoln Highway between Lancaster and Philadelphia.

When I alighted from an automobile at the door-step of the New York University, No. 32 Waverly Place, at 6:30 o'clock, Wednesday evening, October 11, the suspense was over. Great was the satisfaction of having accomplished what I had set out to do. In no other way could I have gained such a knowledge of the country and the people who have made it, and are making it.

Best of all, it gave me a deeper understanding of human nature.

Taking pride in his self-styled "Highwayman" designation links Charlie Brown to those earlier and vagrant free spirits, as well as to my own return to hitch-hiking at a time when I felt myself a social outlaw for refusing to conform in upscale America. The linkage is thus complete from my own perspective.

And it means we now have a lineage and a history — those of us who revel in this wayfaring art. The next step is to find out more about who Charlie Brown was, and what happened to him in the course of his life. Did that venture on an inspirational journey typify, or even contribute to, his later life? Did he ever do more of it, or write anything further about it?

. . . and Here he is!

Freshly revealed from the musty pages of the Sunday, November 12, 1916 edition of the New York World Journal

The First American Hitch-hiker

CHARLES BROWN JR., is the originator of automobile panhandling, the newest game for brake beam tourists.

(well, you'd look a little strange, too, after being buried 88 years)

And what's more … (a shameless hustle)

Dear Reader:

It's a completed book. But not the end of my recorded adventures or anywhere near the sum of amazing synchronicities I've been blessed with. No, indeed … another entire book awaits your reading enjoyment if this one has left you wanting more. An entire book, less the taste of it you've already had in this one (Sections 9 & 10) — there is <u>ten times</u> as much that awaits you, plus a couple dozen pen sketches you are sure to like, as others have.

I'm referring, of course, to <u>Innocence Abroad:</u> <u>Adventuring through Europe at 64 on $100 per week</u>, a 387-page book immediately available, either hard cover or soft, through your local bookstore or online source. They will have a copy printed just for you through Xlibris, the p.o.d. publisher handling it. And it will reward me a bit for your indulgence. (You are aware, I trust, that the proceeds from <u>this</u> book are directed toward the furtherance of the Road Bard Project, a worthy hitch-hiking resource and support function).

Just to add a little spice to my recommendation of <u>Innocence Abroad</u>, I will give away a signed copy of the softcover version to the first five people who can identify <u>both the make and year</u> of the automobile pictured on the cover of this book, the vehicle coming up behind me. If you can correctly specify <u>either</u> the make or the year (but not both) you'll win a $5.00 reduction in the cost of <u>Innocence Abroad</u> — from me, personally, as a rebate, on proof of purchase. But for this second prize, I'll only accept a single (first) entry per person.

Here are two clues that may help by narrowing the range of possibilities: 1) the make has not been in production for well over a half-century; and 2) the year and make together happens to be a street address in Fort Wayne, Indiana, located within a mile from where Charlie Brown, our first American hitch-hiker, began that long-ago road trip (as reported in the Literary Digest article that I've quoted in its entirety in this book's Afterlude closure).

For personal contact regarding the above — or anything else — you can reach me at irvthom1@comcast.net or through inquiry at the Road Bard Project (www.roadbard. org). I am also developing two personal web sites that might be of interest at irv.roadbard.org and www.irvthomas.com

Other (and wider ranging) autobiographical memoir is on the way — you can watch for it under the intended title of <u>A Seasoned Life</u> . . . the Spring Quarter of which I expect to have ready sometime in 2005.

Thanks for the interest you've already shown in my life and work, and may it energize and help to guide your own. As to the road, itself . . . may the fellowship of community ever intrude upon — and be welcomed into — the alienating isolation of the private automobile. And may the vagabond Spirit in all of us forever thrive, and find a fresh host in each arising generation.

Printed in the United States
22414LVS00001B/115-264